Healing Families

*is a Path Book
offering practical spirituality
to enrich everyday living*

*"Your word is a lamp to my feet
and a light to my path."*
Psalm 119:105

"Exploring a wide range of issues such as play, conflict resolution, positive parenting, recovery from addictions, healing trauma, and spirituality, *Healing Families* is a superb roadmap with excellent practical suggestions to nurture healthy family development" — Danny Yeung, MD, Consultant Physician/Psychotherapist, Mount Sinai Hospital; author, *Portrait of the Soul: Spirituality and Character Formation.*

"From her long experience in family therapy and her deep Christian faith, Diane Marshall offers sound advice and concrete hope for struggling families in this perceptive and readable book — an invaluable guide for families, friends, and advisors alike" — Edward W. Scott, former primate, Anglican Church of Canada; former moderator, World Council of Churches.

"In this practical book, Diane Marshall communicates a deep understanding of family challenges and groupings in today's society, and offers clear guidelines for growing authentic relationships" — Maureen McKay, M. Sc., parent and teacher.

Healing Families

Courage and Faith in Challenging Times

Diane Marshall

Path Books
A LIGHT TO MY PATH

ABC Publishing, Anglican Book Centre
General Synod of the Anglican Church of Canada
80 Hayden Street, Toronto, ON, Canada M4Y 3G2
abcpublishing@national.anglican.ca
www.abcpublishing.com www.pathbooks.com

Text set in ITC Legacy Serif Book and CgLisbon
Cover and text design by Jane Thornton
Cover photo: Ryan McVay/Photodisc Green/Getty Images

Library and Archives Canada Cataloguing in Publication

Marshall, Diane, 1944-
Healing families : courage and faith in challenging times / Diane Marshall.

ISBN 1-55126-432-3

1. Family. I. Title.

HQ519.M375 2005   306.85   C2005-901342-7

Contents

Acknowledgements 7

1. Introduction 9

2. Work, Leisure, and Family 21

3. Justice and Change in the Family 35

4. Resolution or Breakup 53

5. Children and Adolescents 69

6. Addiction and Recovery 91

7. Healing the Wounds of Trauma 103

8. Spirituality and Healing 115

for all

who seek to make home and family

a place of peace and love

A Prayer for Home and Family

O God whose desire is
that all the peoples of the world
should be one human family,
living together in harmony,
grant that our home,
by its worship and its witness,
may help to hasten the day
when your will is done on earth
as it is in heaven.

[*Book of Alternative Services,* p. 697]

Acknowledgements

One cannot write a book about families without acknowledging, with appreciation, all those beloved others with whom I have lived various forms of family life for the past six decades. And one cannot be in the practice of therapy for twenty-eight years without owing a debt of gratitude to mentors and colleagues whose lives, wisdom, and skill have blessed my own growth. In particular I wish to thank

Henri Nouwen, Stan Skarsten, Dixie Guldner, James Olthius, and the Reverend Ruth Pogson, each of whom has enriched my life and professional journey.

Archbishop Ted Scott, who so kindly read this manuscript before his sudden death in the summer of 2004, and encouraged me throughout.

My colleagues at the Institute of Family Living, who have been a source of inspiration and conversation as I clarified my ideas: Fran Crabe, Phil Classen, Man-Hon Chu, Orville Green, Suyeon Jin, Brian Maxwell, Nancy Molitz, Cheryl Noble, Lynne Saul, Joan Sinclair, Lindsay Watson, and Danny Yeung.

Friends Penelope Tyndale, Elayne Lockhart, Mary Stewart Van Leeuwen, and the Reverend Carol Finlay, who read drafts and gave invaluable commentary.

Pauline Barrett and Maureen McKay, who gave important feedback on the manuscript.

Gerald and Wynne Vandezande, who have always included my children and me as "extended family."

My sister, Nancy Denham, and my three adult children, Michael and Paul Cowie, and Liz Marshall, who shared love, and allowed me to reflect on the meanings of "family" throughout my own life.

My husband, David Copelin, whose love and support have sustained me as I struggled to put meanings and experiences into words.

Finally, my publisher, Robert Maclennan, who has believed in me and in this book since its inception.

I
Introduction

The world is a source of revelation, not a problem to
be solved.

— W. B. Yeats

A healing journey is dependent on four factors:
Telling the truth (builds a foundation of trust);
Listening to another (builds a bridge of
understanding);
Developing supportive relationships (builds a
sense of belonging);
Regaining a sense of personal dignity (rooted
in forgiveness).

— Author Unknown

Families are facing overwhelming challenges in our post-
modern age. Children are exposed through TV and the Internet
to issues and realities that they may be too young to process,
and to role models that are inappropriate for them. Aging elders
require more care, but no one has time for the slower pace of
life needed by both the very young and the very old. Family members of all ages increasingly suffer inroads on family time, with
a resulting loss of intimacy and connectedness. There is often
no extended family to offer support — no wise uncle or aunt to
consult and little neighbourhood support or other help for over-
worked parents.

Many families are often hard-pressed and at the point of crisis. At times it can seem as if "things fall apart; the centre cannot hold" [*The Second Coming*, W. B. Yeats]. In an age of uncertainty, questions of faith — the meaning and living out of hopefulness, patience, and love; of repentance, forgiveness, and reconciliation — require that Christians re-examine the meaning of our journey, as we face life passages and are challenged to grow.

The particular question of *how* we, as Christians should, respond to social and personal issues, and to complex changes, is a controversial subject. Churches have been known to divide not only over how doctrine should be understood, but also over how faith should manifest itself in works. Growing cultural pluralism in the global village and in Canada requires that we widen our lens and broaden our worldview.

Ultimately we must focus on Jesus himself. Many people seem to compartmentalize life, keeping their faith separate from the lives they are actually leading. But Jesus always did the unusual, and never ignoring anyone, he responded to diverse needs. He responded to the needs of people by teaching and healing publicly and privately. He preached the good news of liberation — of sins forgiven, of new life — to prostitutes and religious leaders alike, often reserving his harshest criticisms for the latter. He healed the lepers who were shunned, and the mentally ill who were outcast.

Jesus' birth, death, and resurrection proclaim to all the earth that there is no separation between body and spirit, that we are enfleshed and embodied persons, created to bear witness in all areas of our life and work to God in whose image we are made. We are not to be subdivided and compartmentalized but are called to be new creatures in Christ, through whom "all things hold together" [Colossians 1:17].

What does this mean for families? We live in a time of immense change in the structure and purpose of family life without the familiar resources and supports. As a result, it is difficult for many Christians to discern the opportunities for their faith to transform family relationships.

Opportunities for growth

Living within a great variety of family forms and emotional systems, family members are challenged to learn to accept one another as having differing needs. Learning communication skills is an essential component of family healing and growth. Developing cooperative rules for resolving conflicts, and fair fighting rules to manage anger in non-destructive ways, are all part of the process.

It is important for parents to understand the developmental stages of their children, for adolescents to understand their own biological changes, and for couples to understand the socialization into gender roles that can inhibit their relationship. And it is important for family members simply to learn to *listen* to one another.

When racism, sexism, homophobia, or some other prejudice wounds a family member's self-esteem, the family needs to *become a place* of healing and hope. When drugs, alcohol, gambling, pornography, or affairs threaten to tear apart the fabric of family relationships, the family needs to *find a path* for healing. When depression, mental illness, physical illness, or accidents impede the functioning of the family, responsible family members need to *seek the help* of others, often including a professional, to ensure appropriate medical treatment and emotional and physical safety for all members of the family.

Likewise, when individuals, couples, parts of families, or whole families consult professional therapists — often referred by a doctor, clergy person, or social worker — they can be aided in their growth and recovery by understanding how their family of origin operated, how their current family relationships are functioning, and how they have come to see themselves as individuals within their family system. This enables people to make conscious and loving choices for change.

Those associated with the family, such as relatives, friends, neighbours, co-workers, and other supporters, can help during challenging times. They cannot formally give professional expertise, but they can be compassionate listeners, encouraging families to seek help if needed. They can also ensure the safety of children, and if need be, report to child welfare authorities when children are at risk or being abused. But most of all they can be a loving and supportive presence, upholding in prayer families who are in crisis and finding concrete ways to show care.

What are "healthy" families?

Healthy families require both flexibility and structure, where core issues of power, control, and intimacy can be resolved in constructive ways. Such families enable openness of discussion, cooperative problem solving, and the freedom for each member to grow and flourish, and to be respected in his or her differences.

In highly functional families, members of the family are able to be comfortable with both their loving feelings and their feelings of annoyance and frustration. As members of an intimate group, each one takes personal responsibility for his or her ambivalent thoughts and feelings. A deep sense of emotional security allows these families to resolve conflicts because they have a sense that "we can work it out." There is a sense of respect that the needs of the self, and the needs of the group, can be resolved in a cooperative way.

"Instead of using emotionally coercive tactics such as intimidation and guilt, healthy families share power and allow for the expression of a wide range of feelings and thoughts. Differences are welcomed as enriching to everyone. As a result, intimacy is safe. Members are free to be both separate and connected" [Philip Classen, *IFL Reflections,* Fall 2003, Institute of Family Living. I am indebted to my colleague, Dr. Classen, for his articulate understanding of what constitutes healthy families and what promotes the healing of families].

Unhealthy families usually display both turmoil and rigidity, where chaotic or authoritarian structures prevent healthy emotional functioning. In such families rules are either non-existent or fixed and non-negotiable. Trust is broken, boundaries of the soul are invaded, and (in violent families) fear and terror reign. Some families are chaotic, lacking rules or clear structure. Others are authoritarian, applying rules that can never be challenged. In both instances, because of the fear that change and loss will prove intolerably painful, the family tends to lack the flexibility or capacity to adapt creatively to new situations.

There are several issues that may develop into crises but that can provide occasions for growth:

- *Narrow definitions of "family" or "marriage"* may constrict how people become intimate partners and raise children, without taking seriously the wide range of intimate connections and family forms that can be understood as mutual commitments.
- *Rigid gender roles* may keep partners from growing in their marriages, and slot children into roles that may not reflect their God-given gifts as persons.

- *Unique personality types* may not be given their due respect if they differ from the family "style" — for example, an extraverted couple may not understand or appreciate their introverted child's need for privacy; an introverted couple may not understand the needs of an extraverted child for a wide range of friends and external activities.
- *Volatile anger and conflict* may be uncontrolled, making everyone emotionally and even physically unsafe; with no "fair fighting rules" and no ability to work through problems, relationships break down and no one can see a way to reconciliation.

How can families find healing?

We are all members of families, and we learn to become social beings through our early experiences of family. Even the most isolated individual can still be understood as a family member. Family ties and the influence of family structures are powerful, even when remote in time and distance. Some people may see themselves as living in splendid (or not so splendid) isolation from a supporting community. An increased awareness of the power and importance of relationships can help such alienated people to achieve hope, healing, and reconciliation, and to gain deeper understanding and more responsible control of our lives.

There are myriad factors that influence our lives. People act and react within larger structures such as partnerships, marriages, families of origin, families of choice, faith communities, socio-economic classes, workplaces, and so on. When such broader circles are added to the potent influences of gender, ethnicity, and genetic, environmental, and medical factors, we can see that the texture and variety of each person's experience forms a complex human tapestry.

Many people suffer from various forms of depression, anxiety, ongoing conflict in relationships, and stress from either severe trauma or the small traumas of everyday life. Many of these difficulties can be helped by discovering how they originated, and how intimacy and respect, power and control have been experienced throughout the various stages of a person's life. So we need to ask questions. During the years of growing up, what strategies did a person learn in order to cope with the many joys and terrors of childhood, adolescence, and adulthood? How did their families, friends, church community, and neighbourhoods help or hinder their growing into mature adults?

Sometimes people seek healing because they are in pain and because denial of that pain is no longer an option. They deserve a lot of credit for survival, for coping, and for the courage to face their own truths despite the difficulty of doing so. It is healing when people gain insight, recapture joy, decide to make changes, and then actually make them. It is healing when people gain (or regain) self-respect, a sense of competence, a sense of adventure in living, and spiritual connection.

A faith journey

It is my hope in writing this book to raise some questions and to share some of my own learnings through thirty years of working with families (and many more of living in family!). Perhaps I may be able to help you, the reader, to identify a range of problems and some possible approaches for healing and restoring family life, so that the experience of others may be a source of Christian hope and inspiration on your own journey.

There is a strong interface between what emerges in doing family therapy and the political and broader social issues of our day. As Christians, we are all called to love justice and to show mercy, especially toward the vulnerable, the wounded, the marginalized. Clergy, pastoral counsellors, social workers, and therapists are among those whose professional calling is to bind up the broken-hearted and to comfort the afflicted. But all of us — friends, relatives, neighbours, teachers, youth workers, co-workers — are called as Christians to "bear one another's burdens" and to support and care for one another, and this includes caring for one another's families.

Many issues that we encounter as ordinary Christians require us to take a prophetic stance, one that challenges oppressive and corrupt power relations. As Dorothy Day, the founder of the Catholic Worker movement, once put it, as followers of Jesus we will often find ourselves "comforting the afflicted, and afflicting the comfortable." Often in our everyday lives we find that what we experience initially as being individual, private, and personal is in fact profoundly linked with the collective, public, and communal. And so there is always a dimension of public justice to our Christian calling to be salt and light. What we often see in microcosm at the personal, family, and relational level is but a reflection of the macro level of faith community, neighbourhood, social institutions, law, and politics.

At a centre such as the Institute for Family Living, where I am the clinical director, psychotherapy is a family affair. We meet a great variety of clients — individuals, couples, families; Christian, Jewish, Muslim, of other faiths, and of no faith community. At first glance, they seem to have little in common except a desire to improve their relationships through therapy. But our clients have a lot more in common than that. No matter what their issues, background, social class, culture, race, gender, or sexual orientation, they all have families of which they are, or have been, a part.

I recognize that, in choosing certain topics, I have had to limit the discussion of others that are equally worthy. I have not looked at some other challenging issues — for example, parenting children with disabilities, dealing with chronic illness and aging, or the increasingly complicated ethical issues surrounding birth and death (when families are confronted with the possibilities of genetic testing and new reproductive technologies, or with questions of assisted suicide or euthanasia). In drawing on my experience as a therapist, I have sought to address topics such as work and leisure, justice issues and family life, conflict resolution and mediated breakup, child and adolescent problems, addiction and recovery, and trauma and healing.

Building healthy families

Listed below are some essential qualities that help build healthy families, enabling members to be both close ("near") and separate ("far") — and to live with integrity within themselves and with others, respecting differences and responding with love.

1. Connectedness *(opposite: alienation)*
a feeling of closeness, of being an integral part of the family, of being cared for in the family

2. Acceptance *(opposite: rejected/judged)*
a sense of being acknowledged, respected, and honoured as a unique member of the family, with one's own thoughts and feelings, gifts and talents, weaknesses and vulnerability

3. Appreciation *(opposite: discounted)*
being acknowledged for our own personal successes, for our contributions to the family

4. Trust *(opposite: fear/mistrust)*
a sense of consistent, predictable attitudes with an emotional foundation of love, respect, and forgiveness among family members

continues on next page ...

---

5. **Truthfulness** *(opposite: denial)*
ability to be open and honest with feelings and information about events in the family

6. **Commitment** *(opposite: indifference)*
members have chosen to make the family a priority in their lives

7. **Flexible rules** *(opposite: rigidity/legalism)*
rules are built on clear values, allowing the family to be collaborative and problem-solving in its approach to change and to life events

8. **Problem solving skills** *(opposite: emotional reactivity)*
good thinking skills are modelled, allowing for members to be proactive

9. **Safety** *(opposite: violation)*
emotional, physical, and sexual security for each member of the family, communicated both verbally and non-verbally

10. **Boundaries** *(opposite: fusion/enmeshment)*
an invisible line between ourselves and others in the family, affirming each one's uniqueness and separateness physically, verbally, emotionally, and spiritually

Rate each of the following ten qualities on a scale of 1 to 5, with 1 being the least present and 5 being the most present. Use column one for your family of origin (the family you grew up in) and column two for the family you currently live with.

Quality	Family of Origin	Current Family
Connectedness		
Acceptance		
Appreciation		
Trust		
Truthfulness		
Commitment		
Flexible rules		
Problem solving skills		
Safety		
Boundaries		

Diane Marshall, 1990

Scattered throughout the book are charts that family members can use to consider important characteristics of their families. At the end of each chapter are references to resources that may help parents and other family members. There are prayers and meditations that may be used for family devotions. And there are some "helpful suggestions" that may spark some discussion and stimulate some movement for change.

It is my hope that this book will provide real encouragement in the complex journey of growing — as members of families — in the love of Christ.

2
Work, Leisure, and Family

In order that people may be happy in their work, these three things are needed: they must be fit for it; they must not do too much of it; they must have a sense of success in it…. [They must have] a sure sense, or rather knowledge, that so much work has been done well, and fruitfully done, whatever the world may say or think about it.

— *John Ruskin*

A household was in distress. The mother, who was the main home organizer and also carried a full-time job, was seriously ill. There was no extended family to help. The father and the four children, whose ages ranged from ten to eighteen, needed to develop a roster of chores in order to help their mother in her recovery.

Initially, no one was willing to make adjustments to help fill the organizational vacuum left by the mother's illness. The father couldn't be home until at least 7:30 every evening from his job in a local factory. The older teens had after-school activities and part-time jobs. The younger children played sports at school, then came home and were used to watching TV. And there was homework to do.

Gradually, and with difficulty, the children picked up some of the household work, and the father did the grocery shopping. With time, the mother recovered, but she was no longer able to work and do the "second shift" of household management, and the family struggled to maintain a more cooperative structure.

This family is not unusual.

Current research on Canadian families

According to the experience of millions of people, and to research done by Canada's Vanier Institute on the Family, the demands of the workplace are a serious threat to the life of contemporary families. Individuals struggle with vocational options. Couples seek to juggle career and marriage. Parents try desperately to balance time with children and the insatiable demands of their employment. Mid-life couples face the prospects and uncertainties of retirement. We are seeing the steady encroachment of the world of work on the time, energy, and commitments of family life.

Until the Industrial Revolution, family life was enmeshed with work life. Early hunter-gatherer societies and later agricultural societies observed divisions of labour that allowed for the care and nurture of children. Extended family networks were always a part of the raising of children and the caring for the sick, the weak, and the elderly. The Industrial Revolution, which spread throughout the world after the eighteenth century, forced people to leave the village in order to seek work in larger urban centres.

Today we read of the "depersonalization" and "alienation" of people living in cities of all sizes throughout the world. Urbanization has undermined the traditional kinship networks that nurtured human life at various stages. Today fewer families live in neighbourhoods where children are known to all and can play freely and safely. Shift work and the breakdown of marriages have further eroded the foundations of neighbourhoods as relatively stable communities.

In Canada, the post-World War Two "single-breadwinner" families have become — of necessity — dual-wage-earning families in order to meet basic expenses such as housing and transportation. Hard-won laws limiting the basic workweek to thirty-five hours are history; some provincial governments have considered extending the permissible workweek by many more hours. What effect would such legislation have on already beleaguered families?

Work and leisure

The demands of the workplace, the attractions of our consumer society, and the breakdown of the extended family have all placed enormous burdens on the shoulders of parents. As work increasingly defines the parameters of self, family, and even friendship, more and more Canadians report fatigue, stress-related illnesses, and a lack of time available to spend with children.

A limited amount of stress helps us to think, cope, and work better. But beyond a certain level, stress begins to fragment us. Hormones flood our system, and our brains go into overdrive. Warning signals of stress-related problems may include anxiety, anger, tearfulness, frustration, forgetfulness, or blocks to creativity. We may experience physical symptoms such as headaches, backaches, or insomnia. When we keep pushing beyond our limits, and fail to take time for relaxation and restoration, we can make ourselves and our families ill.

Family time in contemporary society is eaten away by the demands of work, school, extracurricular activities, television, peer groups, and so on. Quiet moments to connect with each other, to encourage, play with, and listen to each other, to invite friends over; to converse about what each member is learning, are becoming rare.

Likewise, intergenerational times with grandparents, other

relatives, and family friends are disappearing because of our highly mobile culture. Families used to eat several meals a week together, but today family mealtimes are an increasingly rare phenomenon. The Sunday dinner, the Friday evening Shabbat meal, and special events such as birthday and anniversary celebrations helped to keep alive the threads of connection and the bonds of intimacy. As with times of worship, these intentional gatherings — if they are to survive — must be given a high priority, since no longer do they "just happen." We need to plan and set aside time to come together for special family rituals.

Our society's health is linked to the health of the family. But relationships take time and need to be cultivated and nurtured. As such, they require a certain amount of leisure. As a culture, we are currently challenged to re-examine the priorities of work, leisure, and family. With no time for reflective living, there can be a loss of genuine enjoyment of life and of our most intimate relationships. We need to reclaim the habit — indeed, the *commandment* — of a weekly day of rest, a Sabbath.

Question: How to live in time responsibly?

Responses to a time management survey showed that during a lifetime we spend

- 8 months opening junk mail
- 1 year waiting
- 2 years returning phone calls
- 5 years waiting in line
- 1/4 of our life sleeping

Time to listen

Jean Vanier, on the occasion of his seventy-fifth birthday, wrote to members of the worldwide L'Arche communities about the meaning of what he calls "presence." He says this:

> Presence: being present to people who are fragile; being present to one another. To live fully the present moment and not to hide behind some past ideals of future utopia. Our human hearts are thirsting for presence: the presence of a friend; the presence of someone who will listen faithfully, who does not judge but who understands, appreciates, and through love lowers the barriers of inner fear and anguish. This presence implies compassion and tenderness as well as competence. Above all being present to God, listening to God. It is important not to be afraid or to feel paralyzed in front of all that is so painful in our world and in our [families]. We need to discover the presence of God in the actual reality of each day. God is not to be found in the ideal but is hidden in the poverty of the present moment, in all that is broken and inadequate in our [families] and in our own hearts [*Letters to L'Arche*, Fall 2003].

"Presence," then, is the capacity to live in the present moment within our family life, and to be attentive to one another — as couples, as parents with children; to the sick, elderly, and disabled in our midst. Families are the first place where we learn *to be* in the world — to be known, to become, to be understood, to be playful, to be compassionate. When families are stressed and overtaken by the "tyranny of the urgent," there is little time for knowing one another, for listening to one another, for growing emotionally and relationally.

Intimacy should characterize our family relationships, but when we are constrained by work demands, and unable to relax and shift gears at the end of a day, then family relationships suffer. Parents can lose touch with their children. Children often feel alone in the midst of a busy family that makes no time for connections. The elderly and disabled frequently are ignored.

Stephen Covey's Time Matrix

1. Important Urgent	2. Important Not Urgent
3. Not Important Urgent	4. Not Important Not Urgent

[Stephen Covey, *Seven Habits of Highly Effective People* (New York: Simon and Shuster, 1990)]

We might consider Stephen Covey's famous "time matrix," and reflect on how much time we allocate to things that are "important but not urgent" (quadrant two) in our busy schedules. Whether ruled by the urgent, or what seems important in the minute, busy parents frequently have no time to practise the art of what Vanier calls presence for one another or for their children. And how many of us use "not urgent and not important activities" (quadrant four) to tune out or numb out the stressors of the day, without creating space and time for *true reflection*?

If we are to learn to practise the listening skills so essential to the flourishing of relationships, and so critical for the developing young hearts and minds of our children and grandchildren, then we need to intentionally carve out the time for being together. In particular we need to cultivate the art of listening, especially when we are feeling defensive and fearful of losing something that seems important to us. When we can learn to listen and validate another, we *gain* what Vanier calls true "presence." Being with the other and entering into their experience helps us to gain deeper understanding and empathy for our family members.

Sustaining healthy relationships is often a quadrant two issue — "Important Not Urgent." It takes time and patience, and requires good listening.

Good listening recognizes that every human being needs to know:

- I am of worth;
- my thoughts, feelings, and experiences matter; and
- someone really cares about me.

Good listening can help to fulfill these basic needs because through it we act as mirrors for each other and validate each other's lives. Here are four rules of good listening:

- Listen by giving your full attention, without judging or critiquing.
- Listen to both the thoughts and feelings being expressed.
- Listen to the underlying needs being expressed.
- Understand by seeking to put yourself in the other person's shoes.

The liberation of joy

Joy is listed by St. Paul as one of the fruits of the Spirit [Galatians 5:22], but joy is often sacrificed to the "tyranny of the urgent" and to the excessive demands of work on our lives. Joy is elusive; it is more exultant than a sense of well-being, deeper than happiness. Overwhelmed, easily frustrated, often exhausted, and "stressed out," we are all in danger of becoming joyless victims of what the Japanese call "hurry sickness." Children suffer too: child psychologists and educators frequently warn us that our children are overprogrammed and overstressed. Far too often they seem joyless as well.

One person who has embodied reflective, prayerful living in the midst of the "tyranny of the urgent" is Archbishop Desmond Tutu. A personal friend who visited the Tutus at the height of the struggle against apartheid in the mid-1980s reported with amazement that, in the midst of a busy family life and the oftentimes brutal demands of public life, Archbishop Tutu would rise very early in the morning and begin his day with meditation and prayer. This practice has borne remarkable

---

Keys for Good Listening

1. Set a time and place to talk.
This helps to ensure that each of you will be able to communicate and listen well. (Remember to avoid the low blood sugar times. These times are especially risky: 5:00 to 7:00 in the evening or before dinner, and whenever people are tired, especially late at night.)

2. Repeat back (mirror) what the other person said.
This helps to ensure that you understand the concern or issue clearly.

3. Validate what is said.
This does not mean agreeing but, instead, indicating that you understand the meaning of what the other has said and why it makes sense to them.

4. Empathize with the other's feelings.
This helps to show that you understand and care about each other's feelings. The feelings in question may be clear and specific, such as hurt, anger, sadness, disappointment, excitement, happiness, or joy. Or they may be more general and even vague, such as discomfort, uncertainty, frustration, or something quite unclear.

---

fruit in both his personal life and his public life in the South African church and state. Carving out time for renewal and spiritual restoration has allowed this very gifted and faithful Christian leader to respond to the urgent and important demands of his work.

Desmond Tutu has given the world an enduring model of peacemaking. Courageous in the face of the overwhelming systemic oppression of apartheid, and visionary in the process of seeking justice and forgiveness in South Africa's new democracy, Tutu has also struck many with his ebullient spirit, his wonderful sense of humour, and his deep joyfulness. When he speaks, it quickly becomes evident that this joy is grounded in his faith in God's love and mercy, and also in his strong commitment to a view of freedom that encompasses liberation for both victims and oppressors. It is probable that the secret to his joy and his vision is the time he spends in God's presence.

Although in Canada we don't live in a society with the same structural tyranny as South Africa, we are not free from the oppression that robs us of joy. Social injustices, such as homeless people living outside in the cold of winter, children having to rely on food banks for basic nourishment and suffering violence in schools, elderly people living alone in isolated rooms with no visitors, are apt to create us versus them polarizations and reduce people to survival mode.

In families the stress and pace of life create a different kind of oppression. No time for family meals. Few opportunities for tired parents to read bedtime stories to children. Both parents working — usually of necessity — without adequate backup resources in case of illness. Little "couple time" to nourish a couple relationship. The increasing number of single-parent families or families in which one parent travels regularly and the resulting high stress level of the other parent.

Clergy, therapists, family physicians, and other profession-als see daily how stress-related illnesses, chronic sleep deprivation, anger management problems, addictions to alco-hol, drugs, food, and the Internet, contribute to family crises. It can be helpful to do an occasional reality check, using tools such as a stress test (which doctors and therapists can give) that looks at changes and losses over the past year of life, or a time man-agement chart (as mentioned earlier). Such self-care assessments can facilitate reflective living in the family.

Celtic Blessing

Bless to me, O God,
    My soul and my body;
Bless to me, O God,
    My belief and my condition;
Bless to me, O God,
    My heart and my speech;
And bless to me, O God,
    The work of my hands.

Living a reflective life

The challenge to earn more or even just enough money, the lack of extended family supports, and the constant demands of work diminish time available for maintaining family relationships and for the leisure that restores and replenishes our individual and communal souls — such activities as play, friendship, exercise, meditation or worship, attending concerts, walking in nature, adequate sleep, and so on.

Living a reflective life entails changing habits. But chang-ing habits, and creating new patterns in work and home life, requires both time and commitment. The family described in the beginning of this chapter needed to reorganize their priorities. No longer could they expect the mother to run the household and be the hub of the wheel of relationships and communication. Everyone had to make changes, from the father to the youngest child. And it worked. As each person learned to pull his or her weight in the family, the crisis resolved itself and the family became stronger.

The father refused a promotion at work in order to be home at a consistent time, and he learned to be a better listener to both his wife and his children. He also learned to emotionally "shift gears" between work and home so that he was less irritable and more available for relationships. The older children helped their younger siblings with their homework, which eventually strengthened their bonds of affection. With more peace and stability in the family, the mother was able to slowly recover her strength and to take on some responsibilities that she could handle without endangering her health. Family members learned to pray together daily and to draw their strength from God. In this way they were enabled to become open to changes that were ultimately healing.

Noticing the simple things of life and the daily gifts of grace require that we become attentive to the demands being made upon us and learn when to accept and when to refuse them. Archbishop Tutu's time in prayer and meditation every morning allows him to reflect and to receive strength from God. If we take time to allow it, we too may find that *joy*, not stress, begins to rule our lives.

What can we do?

There are things we can all do to be more available to the people we love, and to give the gift of time to our partners, children, parents, and siblings.

Living more reflectively

- We can remember, as people of faith, that we are called to be stewards of *all* our resources (time, talents, money, relationships), and that our calling is to our homes and families and not only to our work.
- We can take time — both individually and as families together — to reflect on the pace of our lives, and examine where and how we actually spend our time.
- We can intentionally share with our families when we are under stress or pressure — at work, at school, in our health, and in our finances — and ask for help and cooperation where possible to solve problems together.
- We can ask our partners, children, and friends to remind us to keep to our priorities so that we do not become workaholics, compulsively driven and unable to reflect or to rest.

Improving communication

- Families can make eating together a priority three or four times a week (with neither telephone and television interruptions, nor other distractions) in order to stay connected and interested in one another's lives and to keep the lines of communication open.
- Parents can volunteer whenever possible to help coach their children's teams, or to go on school trips. Spending one-to-one time with a child can help a parent to understand the child's world.

- Parents can sit with children doing homework, encouraging their learning and working habits, but not doing the work for them.
- All family members can make time for friendships — to visit, call, and e-mail (if a computer is available) those who are precious to us.

Developing cooperative homes

- Families can develop clear rosters of household chores so that everyone contributes to managing the home, and so that housework and the organization of family life does not fall on the shoulders of one person (far too often the mother, or an older sibling).
- Families can play cooperative games instead of competitive ones, so that competition, sibling rivalry, and a winner/loser dynamic doesn't contribute to family stress.
- Families can take the time to celebrate the small things of life and to rejoice with one another in successes and accomplishments.

Study on Canadians and Work: "Voices of Canadians" [reported on CBC's television program *Venture*, 19 January 2003]

133,000 Canadians were surveyed in 2002 on their work/life balance. Here are some of the survey's findings:

- Workweeks of fifty hours or more are common.
- There is high-level use of antidepressants and anti-anxiety medications.
- Absenteeism costs employers about $3 billion annually.
- Flex hours or telecommuting, though often available, are seldom used.
- Many companies pay lip-service to a "family friendly" policy.
- Only 5% of those surveyed said something good about their workplace.
- There has been an 80% increase in fathers using extended parental benefits.
- Caregivers of gravely ill family members need compassionate leave.

3
Justice and Change in the Family

Where, after all, do universal human rights begin? In small places, close to home — so close and so small that they cannot be seen on any maps of the world. Yet they are the world of the individual person; the neighborhood s/he lives in; the school or college s/he attends; the factory, farm, or office where s/he works. Such are the places where every man, woman, and child seeks equal justice, equal opportunity, equal dignity without discrimination. Unless these rights have meaning there, they have little meaning anywhere. Without concerted citizen action to uphold them close to home, we shall look in vain for progress in the larger world.

— *Eleanor Roosevelt*

On moving to a new community, the Smith-Lam family (not their real name) joined the local Anglican church. They were a complex family. The parents had remarried and were from different ethnic backgrounds. They already had children of their own — a preteen older daughter from the mother's previous marriage, and two teenage sons from the father's previous marriage. Into this complex household arrived the wife's eighty-six-year-old widowed mother. This "blended family" was fraught with conflicts. The challenge of ministering to the diverse needs of the family became clear to the youth pastor at the local church when one of the older teenage sons got into trouble with the law for using drugs and was jailed.

——————

Our Christian calling is to model relationships of equality, respect, and dignity in our homes. Major changes both in our own lives and in society may require that we rethink and redefine relationships in marriage and family. This is particularly evident in gender relationships. Paradigm change in families can happen in four areas — *structurally* by a reconfiguration of tasks and roles; *politically* in the balance of power relations; *relationally* in the way individuals interact with one another; and *culturally* in attitudes, beliefs, and patterns of behaviour change that result from cultural shifts.

The global reach of modernity has challenged gender and family relationships in both more and less industrialized nations. One result is the breakdown of economic cooperation between the sexes and between generations. Another is the de-institutionalization of marriage as seen in rising rates of separation and divorce, temporary cohabitation, children born outside marriage, male migration, and family desertion. The juggernaut of economic growth at any cost pays almost no attention to just relationships in family life. Its focus on individual achievement has exacted a terrible price and has failed to take into consideration another paradigm altogether, namely, a *communal* one.

Women and children typically come off badly. The harsh reality is that one in every three children in large Canadian cities is living in poverty and dependent on food banks. Unsurprisingly, there is a strong correlation with the poverty of mothers. Single mothers, urban aboriginals, recent immigrants, the disabled, and elderly women are among those identified as poor. November 2004 marked the fifteenth anniversary of the all-party House of Commons resolution to end child poverty in Canada. Today one in six children still lives in poverty — one million children too many.

Issues of gender and family justice often surface in immigrant families, even beyond the first generation. Our Canadian cities are increasingly becoming home to people from a rich diversity of cultural backgrounds. Toronto, for example, has been named by the United Nations for five consecutive years as the most multicultural city in the world. In such a context, people of different backgrounds struggle to maintain their identities, their cultures, and their family traditions and values in the face of the prevailing Canadian culture and the demands of urban life and market-driven economics.

The effect is often devastating in the lives of women — many may find work in factories and so are co-earners, but they may come home to traditional expectations of domestic labour. Even in two-parent families where young fathers are helping out with family tasks and child-rearing, statistics indicate that mothers working outside the home still bear the larger burden of the "second shift" of housework, with a resulting breakdown in their physical and emotional health. In fact, a publication by the Canadian Advisory Council on the Status of Women, entitled *Women, Paid/Unpaid Work and Stress,* has indicated that this second shift is the most serious health hazard that Canadian women face.

The problem is not restricted to immigrant women. The report looks at the realities of single mothers, as well as immigrant women, in its extensive survey of women's work-related stress and illness. Among single mothers in Canada, 59% live in poverty. Among women over the age of seventy-five, 36% live in poverty.

Among the urban poor, lack of daycare and lack of adequate subsidized housing are seen as major impediments to the improvement of women's and children's situations. The Canadian economy does *not* adequately invest in children. Governments proclaim a "children's agenda" but concentrate on fiscal responsibility, which often means cutting welfare payments, reducing subsidies for daycare spaces, and ending the construction of new housing for low income families. The gap between known need and investment keeps growing. Religious and other civil society institutions are not equipped to fill the breach, and are not as involved as they might be in movements for structural change.

Poverty and families

Recent statistics have shown that, in spite of the federal surplus, food bank use in Canada has continued to rise. "Federal surplus exceeds expectations; food bank use exceeds fears," says Citizens for Public Justice, a Christian public justice organization. CPJ goes on to say that, even though poverty rates have fallen from the depths reached in the mid-1990s, structural poverty rates (based on the use of food banks and other social services) have actually risen.

Food bank use and child poverty are serious social issues, affecting the life of the working poor and those on public welfare. CPJ's Greg deGroot-Magetti writes: "In 2003, while Canada is one of the richest countries in the world — of all time — we cannot ensure that no Canadian child will go hungry. Far from it. Thousands of our neighbours — women, children, and men — during any given month, cannot be sure how they are going to put food on the table" [*The Catalyst*, 2003, vol. 26, no. 6].

I am a member of a congregation that has a large food bank — in fact, the second largest in downtown Toronto, feeding thousands a year. St. Peter's food bank grew in use as the Ontario government's "common sense revolution" withdrew from its social responsibilities in the name of the fiscal bottom line. Such public neglect, as CPJ says, "generated the long lines at food banks that were so familiar to our parents and grandparents.... Successful social policy is about more than accountability and transparency. Successful social policies improve the lives of people and communities. It safeguards the economic well-being of people during vulnerable periods. It strengthens civic vitality and builds more inclusive communities."

When we neglect the public square, and protect only the private sphere of the affluent, all of us suffer. Families suffer alienation. Parents suffer shame. Children suffer hunger. The church is called to speak prophetically to remind us of what constitutes justice for all. Christians are called to grapple with issues of injustice.

Not only do clergy, therapists, teachers, doctors, and other members of the helping professions need to learn more about the effects of global modernity on gender and family relations, but so also do Christian laity. The fact is, families of all kinds today are under siege, facing the consequences that globalization, individualism, and the atomization of our society have produced. Here are a few of the challenges facing families:

- increasing divorce, resulting in the absence of fathers and the pauperization of women and children;
- the complexities of remarried and blended family systems, some of which are same-sex partnerships;
- the disturbing increase in numbers of children in foster care;
- the challenges of immigration, intermarriage between people of different cultures, and the resulting cross-cultural families; and
- a variety of medical-ethical issues ranging from reproductive technologies (such as in vitro fertilization) to questions

of life and death (such as abortion, euthanasia, and embryonic stem cell research).

Family structures in transition

Just as human beings are varied and diverse, so there is no single definition of a household; rather, there is a rich variety of constellations of relationships and commitments. Here are a few examples:

- a member of the "boomerang generation" returning home to parents who were formerly "empty-nesters";
- an immigrant extended family with multi-generational members living together;
- a single adult living alone;
- a single-parent family (usually woman-led) with children and no other significant adult involved;
- a shared custody arrangement of children living equally with both separated (or divorced) parents;
- a nuclear family living, without supports, with a severely disabled child or young adult;
- a gay or lesbian couple in a committed partnership, with or without adopted children; and
- grandparents bringing up grandchildren, often without support from the children's parents or the state.

Family Service Canada's national newsletter, *Let's Talk Families*, frequently looks at family diversity and change and comments on major Statistics Canada studies.

The figures consistently show that the Canadian "family" is undergoing fundamental change. People today are less likely to marry than they were two decades ago. Those who marry tend to do so at older ages. Marriages have also become less permanent; Statistics Canada has estimated that 31% of all marriages will eventually end in divorce.

Divorce and high rates of remarriage mean that children are now more likely to live with a step-parent. In 1995 about half of the 430,000 stepfamilies were headed by common-law couples. Parents in stepfamilies tend to be in their middle years. By contrast, the vast majority — 85% — of lone-parent families are headed by women who tend to be young; over one-third are under age thirty-five.

Marcia Almay of Statistics Canada wrote: "In the 1980s, the number of common-law unions in Canada more than doubled. During the same period, the number of married couples and lone-parent families also rose, but proportionally these increases were much smaller than those for common-law families. As a result, common-law couples made up 10% of all families in 1991." The 2001 Census reports that 20% more Canadian couples than in 1995 are choosing cohabitation instead of marriage. More than half of women in their twenties reported living with a partner before committing to marriage.

"It may be the end of the *Leave It to Beaver* family," said Robert Glossop, director of programs at the Vanier Institute of the Family in Ottawa. "We used to think there was a single portrait of the family in the 1950s; now we have a gallery of diverse images. There's no single portrait" [personal interview with Robert Glossop, December 2003].

Alan Mirabelli of the Vanier Institute noted as far back as September 1989 (in *Let's Talk Families*) that traditional views on marriage are changing and that couples were no longer seeking approval from either the state or church.

How can we design policies for families when we have so much trouble defining them? We used to define family relationships with reference to the formal bonds of matrimony. Now we look at what families do and the commitments of family members to one another. We have come to define family as ... any combination of two or more persons who are bound together by ties of mutual consent, birth and/or adoption or placement and who, together, assume responsibilities for ... and care of ... members.

Marriage and other forms of domestic partnerships are about making a *personal* commitment. Yet David Reed, professor of theology at Wycliffe College in Toronto, is quoted in Toronto's *Metro Today* [18 July 2002] as saying: "These [2001 census] statistics reflect the current suspicion of all institutions, whether political, economical, or religious institutions." Reed observes that today's younger generation have a "take it or leave it mind set" because they are afraid of making the same mistakes their parents did. "They have a higher expectation of marriage but they don't have the confidence that they can actually attain that ... [and] when a relationship starts going sour, the instinct is to end it rather than working through the problems."

In March 2003, Emory University's Center for the Interdisciplinary Study of Religion (CISR) brought together seventy scholars and six hundred attendees for lectures and panel discussions about problems facing contemporary families, and about the role that the "religions of the book" (Judaism, Christianity, and Islam) might play. John Witte, Jr., director of CISR, was quoted as saying that tracking the "intricacies and intimacies" of family life today helps make clear "the principles that will dominate questions about sex, marriage, and family into the 21st century" [Emory University news release, 2 April 2003].

The conference discussed such issues as in vitro fertilization, contraception, adoption, abortion, same-sex marriages, rising rates of divorce, father absence, single unwed mothers, and interfaith unions. Rebecca Chopp, president of Colgate University and a speaker at the conference, had this to say:

To some, the order has become disorder. To some, the oppressive order has been loosened. But family life has never had one name. Family has never had a life in Eden. The greatest family value of all must be continual adaptation.

She went on to describe the shift from fixed, rigid systems, to open, permeable boundaries. Chopp challenged her audience about the future:

The birth control pill was a watershed moment. Contraception and reproductive technology uncoupled sex and marriage and family. The "ands" became much more ambiguous ... we used to debate property rights, now we worry about the ownership of eggs and sperm ... how do we shape the social order if the family isn't at the center?... questions about abuse, economics, "quality time" for parenting, and the presence of fathers will continue to occupy us ... but beyond the religious, legal, biological, and cultural codes that ground families, the meaning of family must be re-imagined [Emory University news release, 2 April 2003].

Many Christians have taken up the cry for justice in the changing family. Christian feminist scholar Mary Stewart Van Leeuwen, in *After Eden: Facing the Challenge of Gender Reconciliation,* and in *My Brother's Keeper,* writes passionately about the ongoing patriarchal entrenchment of our culture, mother-headed post-divorce households, and the pauperization of women. Her observations and conclusions concur with the well-documented longitudinal studies of American post-divorce life described in the work of Judith Wallerstein and Sandra Blakeslee in their books *Second Chances: Men, Women, and Children a Decade After Divorce,* and *The Unexpected Legacy of Divorce: A 25 Year Landmark Study.*

The church and family healing

Not only are family relationships varied and complex, but so also are the ways in which they break down. Educational and family support programs run by churches help to alleviate the scope of these problems, but dedicated clergy and lay workers report serious family life issues, such as

- families seeking healing from multigenerational patterns of addictions, violence, or sexual abuse;
- family members divided over the controversial question of "recovered memories" of abuse;
- families in crisis because a member suffers a mental illness so serious that he or she can no longer live at home. All too often governments have ceased to provide suitable housing or care for such people; instead, they release psychiatric patients into a non-existent "community";
- families who lose a teenager to the drug culture and are devastated to find their son or daughter has become a "street kid";
- families of the working poor, squeezed out of the house ownership and rental market, often having to rely on shelters and food banks to survive;
- families with a sole parent, left abandoned after a divorce, and children suffering untold repercussions;
- families composed of same-sex couples longing for their unions to be blessed by their faith community;
- families unable or unwilling to support a teenage girl struggling with whether to have an abortion or to bear a child;
- families who lack adequate *child* care for parents working outside the home;
- families lacking adequate *elder* care, creating great stress for what has come to be called the "sandwich generation," struggling to raise a younger generation with inadequate time or resources to care for their aging parents.

At the 1987 Singapore Consultation of the International Family Network, to which I was a Canadian delegate, delegates from every province of the Anglican Communion described family violence as a serious problem. Spousal abuse (physical, emotional, sexual) was understood to be widespread and had no cultural or geographic boundaries. Child abuse, however, was seen as a more horrific problem, and perceived by our sisters and brothers in the developing world as being endemic to the more affluent West, who they believed had long since devalued children and family life.

In particular, child sexual abuse and the dispersion of child pornography (subsequently more widespread with the advent of the Internet) was perceived to be a sign of the decadence of capitalism, infiltrating developing countries through sex tourism and resulting in increased trafficking of poor children and youth in the sex trade. In all the discussions of the consultation, both formal and informal, concern about family violence was central. How can we, as Christian followers of the Prince of Peace, be agents of reconciliation and justice-seekers in both our personal and our church families? The issues surrounding family violence bring together issues of gender justice, the rights of children, sexual ethics, and the meaning of Christian peacemaking.

Since that consultation, the plight of child soldiers, child labourers, and child sex-trade workers has increasingly come before the public eye. In 2000 Canada hosted the UN Conference on Children of War and signed the declaration banning child soldiers. Canada has also introduced legislation that will allow our government to prosecute pedophiles accused of using children in the sex trade at home and abroad. Numerous warnings are publicized for parents to beware of and to monitor their children's use of the Internet, outlining the dangers of predators contacting children and youth through chat lines.

Canada has laws and social services to prevent and assist healing from violence and sexual abuse within families and communities. Child Welfare authorities are meant to implement child protection laws and support vulnerable families in order to help prevent child abuse. For seniors there is a government program — Strategy to Combat Elder Abuse. Anglicans have been prominent among those who have advocated for laws to address all aspects of violence against women, children, and the elderly.

In the wake of sexual abuse scandals reported in churches in all parts of the country, the Anglican Diocese of Toronto in 1990 developed one of the church's first sexual misconduct policies. This policy highlighted our Christian calling to be a healing and restorative community, and became an inspiration for other dioceses and denominations to follow suit. Likewise, the Anglican Church has consistently raised the issue of spousal abuse and promoted a position of zero tolerance for violence within the family.

It is now common *to pray* for any who are victims of violence or abuse in their homes, *to preach* about non-violence in the family, and *to teach* through ministries for children and youth, and in marriage preparation and enrichment, that our calling in Christ is to model relationships of equality, respect, and dignity within our homes. Teaching concrete skills such as anger management, conflict resolution, and good listening skills, as well as helping children learn not to bully others or stay silent when abuse occurs, is part of helping the next generation to become peacemakers at home and in the world.

Our Christian calling to family justice

The often controversial and always soul-searing task of restoring justice to family life — our own family or someone else's — requires both a compassionate worldview and a supportive community so that we are neither defeated nor burnt out by the work involved. But we live in a consumer culture of greed and covetousness, where people as well as things are used and discarded. The question for many, Christians sadly included, is not "How can I be of service?" but "What do I get out of it?" As

---

The story goes that some time ago a man punished his five-year-old daughter for wasting a roll of expensive gold wrapping paper. Money was tight and he became upset when the child used the gold paper to decorate a box to put under the Christmas tree. Nevertheless, on Christmas morning the little girl brought the gift to her father and said, "This is for you, Daddy." The father was embarrassed by his earlier overreaction, but his anger flared again when he opened the present and found the box was empty. He spoke to her in a harsh manner: "Don't you know, young lady, when you give someone a present there's supposed to be something inside the package?"

The little girl looked up at him with tears in her eyes and said, "Oh, Daddy, it's not empty. I blew kisses into it until it was full." The father was crushed. He fell on his knees and put his arms around his little daughter, and asked her to forgive him for his anger.

An accident took the life of the child only a short time later, and it is told that the father kept that gold box by his bed for the rest of his life. Whenever he was discouraged or faced difficult problems, he would open the box and take out an imaginary kiss and remember the love of the child who had put it there.

In a very real sense, each of us as human beings has been given a golden box filled with unconditional love and kisses from our children, partners, family, friends, and God. Such a gift is more precious than all the things money can buy, and we need to remind ourselves to treasure it above all else.

— *Author unknown*

followers of Jesus, we are challenged by Christ's example of compassion when confronted with the twofold calling of pursuing, both in private and in public, the act of maintaining faithful relations with others and pursuing justice for all.

As Christians in a society devoted to instant gratification, we do not find it easy to practise the kind of self-denying discipleship needed to love our neighbour. When the neighbour is someone we live with — a member of our own family — the task may be even more challenging.

In the private sphere, maintaining relationships of fidelity takes patience and commitment to work things through together, not easy recipes or quick fixes. In the public sphere, as the church seeks to pursue justice in the context of a globalized economy, we in the pews are frequently embarrassed by child poverty in our own backyard, as well as the evils of child labour and sweatshops in distant places that sustain the fashion industry and other aspects of our consumer lifestyle. In the realm of nature, as the ecosystem is being destroyed by corporate exploitation, our aboriginal brothers and sisters call us to be stewards of the creation and we ignore them at our peril.

The gospels record that Jesus welcomed the children, the "little ones," and held them up as role models of faith. But children need households in which to be born, to grow, and be nurtured. We must ask ourselves, "What does it mean for us to do justice and to seek mercy for God's little ones?" These children are in our midst — in our families, churches, classrooms, neighbourhoods, dormitories, reformatories. And within each one of us there lives the child we once were. *Here is where the public and the private interface.*

We are called to love our neighbour as ourselves, but if we ignore our own pain and do not learn compassion for our own brokenness, then often we cannot be truly merciful to others.

We hide, we erect defences, we avoid getting involved. When we "walk by on the other side of the road" and ignore the call to be like the good Samaritan, showing compassion for our neighbour [Luke 10:25–37], we do so because to get close to someone else's pain brings us too close to our own. We are terrified of our own pain, afraid to face the shame that often binds us.

From a Christian point of view, the family is more than a basic social unit. It is a sphere where God is at work in us, shaping and moulding us so that we may share Christ's life of love. If in the family we seek to be "rooted and grounded in the love of Christ," as St. Paul's letter to the Ephesians puts it, we can learn to be people who grow in love and bring love to a wider community. These are the "family values" that count.

Jesus himself never held up one exclusive model of family structure. In fact, in Mark 3:31–35, where it is recorded that his mother and brothers came to see him, Jesus's response shows that he includes many others in how he defines family. "Whoever does the will of God," he explains, "is my brother and sister and mother." From then on, kinship through blood was enlarged to include all those who chose to do the will of God.

The early church community behaved like a kinship group, eating together in various homes and sharing their possessions in common. The family, then, is an intentional community within which the biological family, the adoptive family, and the group made a family through "adoption" by faith are important in the raising and nurture of children. The call to love one another means that we treat each other like kin, in equality and with respect for the dignity of each, so that both individuals and families may thrive.

In other words, Christian believers are called to realize the presence of God in our midst and in one another, and to value and support those characteristics of community that are foundational to healthy families (see chart in the Introduction, p. 17). Such characteristics make it possible for all people — whether heterosexual or homosexual, male or female, old or young, rich or poor, healthy or disabled, black, red, brown, yellow, or white — to sustain relationships of intimacy, connectedness, and nurture, providing opportunities for creativity, and fostering mutual support and interdependence.

A welcoming community of faith makes room for the complex structure of the Smith-Lam family, described at the beginning of this chapter. The bonds of love and faithfulness can be encouraged in the Smith-Lam family by the support and care of their church during the difficult months of court proceedings, when their son can receive pastoral visits in prison and his parents and siblings can be upheld in prayer.

Biblical faith informs us that our goal is the flourishing of persons, individually and communally, and households are foundational communities. Jesus said, "I call you not servants, but friends" [John 15:15]. Our task then, as his friends in an age when families are under pressure, is to re-imagine and re-create household communities as the embodiment of justice and love.

What we can do

Here are some suggestions for creating just household structures, to encourage and sustain family community and cohesiveness:

- Everyone (adult and child, male and female) shares in the maintenance, cleaning, and care of the home and garden. Housework and yard work are not subject to gender or age divisions of "Mom's" versus "Dad's" jobs. Such cooperative care of the household teaches a basic sense of fairness.

- Everyone (male and female, young and old) learns to care for the weaker or most vulnerable members of the family, including the pets. Care-giving is not merely "women's work."
- Everyone has an age-appropriate share, however small, of the family finances, to spend as they see fit, and to save for special occasions or gifts. Money is to be shared, not possessed by only the major wage earner(s).
- Everyone shares in an age-appropriate way in major decisions that affect the family as a whole — moves, holidays, school events, etc.
- Informal but regular family meetings allow for open communication and resolution of conflicts or differences among family members, and help to keep relationships open and growing.
- Professional help is enlisted when anger management and conflict resolution become problems, and before these escalate into family violence, whether spousal abuse, elder abuse, child abuse, or sibling abuse.
- Everyone learns to accept people as they are, refusing to isolate or ostracize a family member because of some difference (for example, someone being gay, or wanting to leave home sooner or stay home longer than their siblings have, or suffering a physical or intellectual disability, or being unable to complete school, or being depressed).

Resources

Family Service Canada. September 1989. *Let's Talk Families*. Ottawa. *(For further analysis, see <www.familyservicecanada.org>.)*

Lowe, Graham S. 1989. *Women, Paid/Unpaid Work, and Stress*. Canadian Advisory Council on the Status of Women: University of Alberta.

Marshall, Diane. 2003. "Violence Against Children," in *Anglican World*; no. 111, Michaelmas. London: The Anglican Communion Office.

Stewart Van Leeuwen, Mary. 2002. *My Brother's Keeper: What the Social Sciences Do (And Don't) Tell Us About Masculinity*. Downer's Grove, Illinois: Intervarsity Press.

Stewart Van Leeuwen, Mary; Annelies Knoppers; Margaret L. Koch; Douglas Schuurman; Helen M. Sterk. 1993. *After Eden: Facing the Challenge of Gender Reconciliation*. Grand Rapids, Michigan: Eerdmans.

Vanier Institute of the Family. 1999. *Transitions*. Winter, vol. 29, no. 4. *(Also see <www.VIFamily.ca>.)* Personal interview with Dr. Robert Glossop, executive director, 3 December 2003.

Wallerstein, Judith S., and Sandra Blakeslee. 1989. *Second Chances: Men, Women, and Children a Decade After Divorce*. Boston: Houghton Mifflin.

4
Resolution or Breakup

If you trust, you will be hurt,
but if you don't trust, you will never learn to love.
— *Gandhi*

The love of truth drives us from the human world to God;
the truth of love sends us back to the human world.
— *William of Thierry, twelfth-century mystic*

———————

The twentieth century, the most violent in human history, has ended. As we begin the twenty-first century, we need to remember that God calls us to be peacemakers. We don't have to be professionals to help others resolve conflicts and build bridges toward peace. Helping others resolve conflicts with themselves, their partners, children, parents, colleagues, or neighbours, requires patience, compassion, faith, and often "tough love." As we ourselves lay down our "swords" and turn anger, mistrust, and strife into the "ploughshares" [Micah 4:3; Isaiah 2:4] of mutual understanding and cooperation, we feel the potential of transformation and hope.

For many people, profound reconciliation becomes possible; for others, a mediated resolution provides a kind of truce. The day-to-day ways in which we help children be friends, reduce sibling rivalry, work cooperatively in our workplaces, and seek deeper understanding with partners and friends who have wounded us, stretch us all to grow in our understanding of the psalmist's vision of a time in which "justice and peace shall embrace" [Psalm 85:10]. Although we cannot realize this vision completely (that is ultimately God's work), we can achieve substantial healing in ways that are compatible with it.

Why do conflicts occur?

In any relationship, community, or workplace, conflicts are an inevitable outcome of personal interaction. The family is a complex community consisting of people living together and relating over time, so it's hardly surprising that a variety of conflicts arise. The following are examples.

Misunderstandings. These occur when one person doesn't say explicitly what she or he thinks or feels, and the other draws conclusions or makes assumptions rather than asking questions and clarifying. With the stresses of life and the varied needs of people, it is easy to become so rushed that we fail to check out what someone really means.

Hurt feelings. It is natural to be hurt by comments that convey insult, blame, or fault-finding in a manner that is destructively critical. Being ignored can also be very hurtful. Learning how to give honest and constructive feedback that does not destroy another person is a skill we can all learn. It is part of the biblical injunction to "speak the truth in love" so that we can grow relationally and individually.

Defending turf. We naturally become defensive as a result of feeling "invaded" or when another's communication seems adversarial. Insensitivity to another's boundaries or time constraints can contribute to this kind of conflict. Instead of being oppositionally competitive in our attitudes or behaviour, we need to learn how to build a bridge, moving toward a place of peace (for example, "Can we solve this together?"). The Christian life is not a "zero-sum game," in which one person's gain is another person's loss; it is a life in which we all grow, individually and as groups.

Not feeling heard. Sometimes it appears that the other person is refusing to listen, or is responding from a "yes but" stance. Often that person can't or won't listen, or becomes unavailable to talk either now or later. It may be necessary either to set another time to resolve the issue, bring in a third party to mediate, try writing a letter, or simply accept that only limited communication is possible with the person — at least on that particular issue at this particular time.

Escalations. These occur in families when there are insufficient or unclear rules, or no structural framework or protocol, for resolving issues. For example, without a process for conflict resolution, disputes can escalate seriously. For this reason, it is helpful to develop "fair fighting rules," which clarify and enable a creative process for resolving conflicts in the home. Such a process needs to be solution-focused and non-coercive. One helpful model of conflict resolution process is shown in the box. (Please see next page.)

Recipe for fulfilling marriages

For an intimate partnership to be truly fulfilling and long-lasting, at least four ingredients are necessary:

- a clear personal *identity* for each partner (for example, each partner, as much as possible, needs to be comfortable in his or her own skin);
- a clear *vision* for the relationship, setting goals that include the possibility of growth and change in the various stages of the marital life cycle;

Ten steps to resolving conflict

1. Set aside a time and place for discussion.
- Allow at least thirty minutes.
- Choose a time when all parties can be relaxed and not interrupted.
- Establish a process for assuring that one person doesn't dominate or interrupt (for example, a "talking stick" held by each person as they speak in turn).

2. Define the problem or issue of disagreement.
- Deal with only one issue at a time.

3. Be honest about how each of you contributes to the problem.
- Without blaming, separately list the things you and the other person do that contribute to the problem.

4. List past attempts to resolve the issue that were or were not successful.
- Resist the temptation to dwell on past failures and cast blame.

5. Brainstorm — list all possible solutions.
- Pool new ideas and try to find several alternative solutions to the problem.
- Include solutions that may have worked in the past in other areas.
- Do not judge or criticize any of the suggestions at this point.

6. Discuss and evaluate these possible solutions.
- Be as objective as you can.
- Use reflective listening (telling the other what you've heard), and discuss how useful and appropriate each suggestion might be for resolving the disagreement.

- Be sure to listen to each other's feelings around each proposed solution, because the feelings behind the words are as important (or more important) than the words themselves.
- Clarify that solutions do not require lopsided sacrifices from one or more members of the group.

7. Agree on one solution to try.
- Select one solution that everyone agrees to use on a trial basis.

8. Agree on how each person will work toward that solution.
- Be as specific as possible, and refer to concrete behaviours, not generalities (for example, "Joe will vacuum the house every week by Saturday at 7:00 p.m." or "Sarah will wipe the kitchen counters every day after each meal," not "We will keep the house clean").

9. Set up another meeting to discuss your progress.
- Set a time and date within the next week.
- Don't be too legalistic; if circumstances occasionally interfere with one person's getting a job done, be understanding and help them get back on track and on schedule as soon as possible.

10. Reward each other (through recognition) as you contribute to the solution.
- Show appreciation and praise efforts made when you see that the other person is making a contribution toward the solution.

- a *mutual commitment* to love and fidelity; and
- a *willingness* to work together to achieve personal and relational peace.

A mutual decision to seek understanding, and willingness to learn the skills needed to face challenges together, are necessary ingredients for growth and healing within an intimate relationship. The commitment to one another must be firm as a couple seeks to work things through. But other ingredients may include the presence of a competent therapist to work with them at one or more periods of their marital journey, and the support of a community (family, church, friends) to encourage growth and resolution. At such times, God's grace is often mediated through the love of others, as well as through the regular practices of worship, prayer, meditation, and study.

The role of faith in healing a marriage

Until the mid-twentieth century, the church allowed members to divorce, or divorce and then remarry, only under very exceptional circumstances. Now, in an age of divorce, the church must work to strengthen marriages in the ways noted above, while also embodying the good news of forgiveness and restoration, of new beginnings and renewed hope for those who experience shame and failure after a broken marriage. Some faith communities are more successful at this than others. Many have grief groups, or programs in recovery from divorce, that include separated and divorced members of the congregation. It is important that the grief of children be acknowledged, as well as that of their parents, when intimate partnerships are incapable of reconciliation.

But if reconciliation is to occur, certain conditions are crucial. Many people of faith report the following to be important as they seek to heal their relationship:

- the *courage* to face their problems openly, without denial or avoidance;
- the *strength* to face their need to change, and the *grace* to learn how;
- the *love* to sustain them even in the darkest times, such as family crises, death, job loss, illness; and
- the *commitment* to God's calling to their vocation of marriage.

Many couples have had little or no experience of Bible study or prayer in their relationship, and many say that when a marriage is in crisis they have no spiritual nurture. One partner may engage in spiritual practice, such as joining a prayer group, while the other offers passive resistance amounting to sabotage. Many couples, although they worship together, are really out of fellowship in a spiritual and emotional sense with one another, and this exacerbates the difficulties they face in the course of their shared life.

Many Christian counsellors try to encourage couples to find a way to pray together and to have their life informed by regular scripture reading so that their emotional and family life is nourished by their faith. As partners learn to listen to one another, to truly hear the deepest needs and longings of the heart of their spouse, a window often opens for deeper communion, and fresh air enters to revitalize the marriage. As new skills and healthier relational patterns are developed, counselling may be needed less frequently.

Often couples divorce who otherwise could have restored their relationships, had the appropriate help been available. As a result, many children are torn between two separated parents and could be helped if their parents had a clearly defined parenting plan that outlines a process for resolution of difficulties and does not put the children in the middle. Parents who divorce need to realize that children have the need and right to love both their parents, and (unless prohibited by court order due to violations such as physical or sexual abuse) they need to feel connected to each of their parents. If and when remarriage or new partnerships occur, old loyalties must be preserved along with new ties.

Sadly, some family relationships cannot be restored or healed. Irreconcilable situations may be robbing the relationship of God's call to life. Sometimes it is because of hardness of heart, an unforgiving spirit, a refusal to walk the path of reconciliation. Sometimes it is because physical or emotional abuse cannot and should not be tolerated any longer, and the relationship needs to end.

Sometimes there are events external to ourselves or destructive to family life that undermine a marriage. These include war, natural disasters, physical or psychiatric illness, substance abuse, pornography and other addictions — all of which can thwart reconciliation from occurring. At such times we need to depend on God's grace to move forward, and to rebuild our lives and the lives of our children. In order to do so without being bound by guilt or shame, we may need to seek spiritual, as well as psychological, counselling.

Marriage counselling

Couples enter into family or marital therapy with a wide array of issues. There may be conflicts with parents or grandparents from a family of origin. There may be conflicts with children or between the couple themselves, or conflicts related to the employment that one or the other engages in. No couple exists as an isolated unit, and a trained marriage and family therapist will seek to explore the relationships and connections that form the landscape of the couple's life.

Many couples seek help because one or both are in emotional distress. This can have any number of causes — a vocational transition or job loss, a health crisis (for example, diagnosis of cancer or infertility), problems with aging parents or the death of a parent, persistent rage and violence, alcohol or drug abuse, an affair (sexual and/or emotional), or problems with children from a former marriage.

Sometimes couples experience positive life changes that are also stressful, such as a geographical or vocational move, the birth of a child (with the resulting sleep deprivation and other adjustments), children leaving home (or returning), or the marriage of an adult child. Occasionally couples have to face life events that are traumatic because they are unexpected, such as the disappearance or death of a child, the birth of a seriously disabled child, a car accident, bankruptcy, or the diagnosis of chronic disease (for example, diabetes or multiple sclerosis).

Many churches provide a real sense of community at times like these. However, a crisis in the couple's normal support system (for example, a schism in their church or the divorce of close friends) may also be a source of distress that can send couples into therapy.

No single life-cycle event may require the help of a therapist, but if, in combination with other events, there is cumulative stress, then the couple's relationship may be helped by professional support. For example, if one partner is diagnosed with cancer at the same time as children begin to leave home, and the person's aging parents need help to face moving into a retirement residence, that person may be overwhelmed and depressed. A therapist could advise the other partner how to show more empathy and practical support at such a time, and could provide additional emotional support and communication skills training for both members of the couple.

Many couples seek counselling because of infidelity of one or both partners. Infidelity breaks a sacred bond based on an exclusive commitment to another to love and care for the other. Marriage relies on a culture of fidelity. But because we live in a consumer culture that exalts personal choice and pleasure seeking, a marriage covenant is often seen as a contract that easily can be cancelled. Whether straight or gay, couples who make a sacred bond often need help and support to maintain their covenant, and to develop courage and forgiveness to rebuild the relationship if that covenant has been broken by infidelity.

Many couples seem to manage life just fine until there is a buildup of stressors that trigger withdrawal or abusive or acting-out behaviours, and then the couple loses touch with each other. Other couples, plagued by responsibilities or issues they brought into the marriage (for example, a history of childhood abuse, children from a previous marriage, poor anger management skills, patterns of chronic workaholism, etc.) may never learn the skills necessary to cope with managing stress or money or conflict, or to make cooperative decisions.

Some couples become shipwrecked on the shoals of different philosophies of relationship fidelity or the meaning of commitment. Whatever the origins, dysfunctional patterns can develop and, in spite of a couple's faith, their emotional and relational "dance" lacks the necessary choreography to meet the challenges of life together.

Family mediation

A couple called my colleague, who is a family mediator, asking for help to end their marriage and protect their children. Both people of faith, they had three children, ages four, six, and eight. Each partner had sought personal counselling, but the husband's chronic workaholic patterns and heavy drinking continued to create much distress in the couple's relationship, and in his parenting of their children. In spite of efforts to change these patterns, the husband finally realized that he didn't want to give the time needed to repair the marriage. However, he was determined to be as good a parent as possible. After speaking with his priest, he was persuaded to seek a less adversarial approach to his wife in terminating the marriage, and he phoned and made arrangements for both of them to see a family mediator.

Adversarial legal justice may be useful in some situations, but not when dealing with failed intimate relationships. When children are involved, the adversarial approach encourages everyone to think in terms of "good" and "bad" people — heroes and villains — not useful categories for either parents or children who, like all of us, represent a complex mix of motives and behaviours, both positive and negative, conscious and unconscious. Successful mediation saves time and money, and makes it easier for separated couples to co-parent and to talk with each other civilly.

Family mediation is a constructive, non-adversarial way to resolve family and parenting issues that inevitably accompany separation or divorce. It can help to reduce the pain, the time, and the expense of finding solutions. A professionally trained, impartial mediator assists the couple and other involved family members to define new relationships, roles, and responsibilities.

While family mediation is not itself therapy, it is a therapeutic means of resolving contentious family issues. It provides couples the opportunity to face each other with less risk and vulnerability and to identify and address unresolved conflicts that can get in the way of negotiating a successful post-marriage agreement. When there is not a gross imbalance of power (for example, financially) or a history of violence and serious abuse of a spouse or children, then mediation is often a useful process for resolving and ending a marriage conflict.

For example, family mediation can help to determine

- how and when to separate;
- how to let go of the past and to develop an effective parenting plan for the children;
- how to address and resolve difficult financial issues;
- how to make appropriate personal decisions;
- how to reduce stress, conflict, and the threat associated with litigation; and
- how to ensure private and confidential resolution of contentious issues.

Mediators can also help to create a written Memorandum of Understanding outlining an agreement that can then be legally finalized by lawyers.

Lawyers, clergy, social workers, psychologists, and marriage and family therapists who refer their clients to a trained mediator can help people in crisis deal with the overwhelming transition that separation and divorce can represent. During the mediator's temporary intervention, people benefit from the continued involvement of their primary helping professional. The overall goal is to help divorcing couples move out of the role of partners while continuing to focus on their enduring relationship as parents for their children.

Mediation is a process, but it is not the same as therapy. It is also not suitable for everyone. A mediator must assess such factors as

- the parties' consent to the mediation process;
- whether or not the parties can talk to each other (with the mediator's assistance) in a safe environment;
- the level of commitment of both parties to settle the issues;

- the level of clarity and understanding of these issues possessed by both parties;
- the parties' ability to state their needs and interests;
- the parties' understanding of their basic rights and responsibilities under the law; and
- whether there are any factors (such as domestic violence) that would make the mediation process difficult or impossible.

How does mediation work?

In mediation two or more people work with a more objective third party, a mediator, to resolve the issues between them by consensus. Similar principles govern both family and small business mediation, although the process may be somewhat less formal in family situations.

Much (though not all) family mediation deals with the aftermath of marital breakdown. When partners, married or not, decide to separate and live apart, conflicts often arise concerning financial support, the nurturing of children, and the division of property. Traditionally such issues were worked out through the legal system, which pits former partners against each other as adversaries. This approach can make things worse rather than better. Mediation is a rapidly growing alternative to litigation, and its popularity is easy to understand.

Mediation allows the parties themselves to determine what issues need to be addressed and in what order. It fosters a sense of cooperation between the parties rather than conflict, an obvious virtue when children are involved. A trained mediator assists the parties to work out agreements that are imaginative yet practical, and that meet the unique needs of the people and relationships involved. Moreover, mediation is time effective and comparatively inexpensive.

Virtually any issue is appropriate for mediation, as long as all parties agree to discuss it in the context of a clearly defined and consistent process. A common issue in family breakup is the development of a "parenting plan" for children. This may include custody, access, support for children and/or spouses, disposition or handling of property, care of the elderly, parent-child conflicts, and also how to navigate the practical effects of different values.

My colleague Joan Sinclair says,

> The details may vary, but the basic structure of the process is pretty consistent. The parties and I will meet together in my office, usually five or six times for ninety minutes each time. Ideally the parties work together, face to face, to negotiate an agreement. Sometimes I meet individually with each party. Where face-to-face meetings are inappropriate, I can do "shuttle diplomacy" back and forth between the parties, who may never be in the same room.
>
> Where children's needs are at issue, and if they and their parents agree, I may meet with them individually, without the adult parties being present. In a conflict between a parent and an older child, the child is a party and needs to be present at joint mediation sessions.

What does the mediation process focus on?

Mediation focuses on the needs and interests of the parties and their children. People often begin a mediation with a fixed, firm, "bottom line" position. After discussing with the mediator and with the other party why that particular position is so important to them — that is, what needs that bottom line meets — they may discover that there are alternative ways of meeting those needs, while also meeting the needs of the other party. No one is coerced into anything; all decisions are reached by consensus. "I don't make any decisions for my clients," says Joan Sinclair. "They make the decisions together, and they craft the agreement between them. I facilitate the process, and I counsel them to consult with others, such as their respective lawyers, accountants, therapists, and family members."

This may be the way that living at peace with one another is achieved for those who are painfully ending a marriage. Mediation may be a kind of peacemaking, and its fruit may be the flourishing of the children or others in the family who feel at least temporarily dismembered at the finality of family breakdown and divorce.

The role of the faith community

The church can play a supportive and healing role in the lives of family members who are going through the often excruciating pain of divorce. By resisting making judgements or taking sides, except in situations when one or more members are in need of safety, the church community can be a stabilizing help to children, a kind of extended family during a time of upheaval. It is important for churches to have fellowship groups that are not couple-centred, so that someone going through marital breakdown can have a place of support and acceptance.

The church is called to offer marriage, couple, and family education programs, so that the risk of breakup is reduced. Yet at the same time, the church needs to work to minimize damage and maximize healing in those cases where reconciliation is not possible. Encouraging a mediated process would be one such peacemaking effort.

Resources

For Children

Emily Menendez-Aponte. Illustrated by R. W. Alley. 1999. *When Mom & Dad Divorce: A Kid's Resource*. Indiana: Abbey Press.

About Children

Wallerstein, Judith S., Julia M. Lewis, and Sandra Blakeslee. 2000. *The Unexpected Legacy of Divorce: A 25 Year Landmark Study*. New York: Hyperion.

About Child Support Guidelines

Federal Child Support Guidelines: call 1-888-373-2222.
Web site: <http://canada.justice.gc.ca>.
Provincial Child Support Guidelines Ontario web site:
<http://www.attorneygeneral.jus.gov.on.ca>.
Choose "How May We Help You?"

Information on Divorce Law

Write Department of Justice Canada, 284 Wellington Street, Ottawa, Ontario K1A 0H8, or visit the Department of Justice web site: <http://canada.justice.gc.ca>.

Information for Women

A Snapshot of Family Law Proceedings; Custody and Access Issues When You Have Experienced Abuse; Getting Your Possessions Back. Pamphlets available from National Association of Women and the Law, 1 Nicholas Street, Suite 604, Ottawa, Ontario K1N 7B7.
Telephone 613-241-7570. E-mail: nawl@ftn.net

Emergency Resources for Children

For information and/or help for children who may have been abused, your local Child Welfare authorities will help you. Consult the emergency numbers at the front of the telephone directory, or call the operator for assistance.

5
Children and Adolescents

Tell me and I may forget;
Explain to me and I may remember;
Involve me, and I will understand.

— *Anonymous*

———

After a serious suicide attempt, nine-year-old "Jessica" was admitted to hospital for in-patient psychiatric treatment. She had many problems. Besides feeling that her life was not worth living, she was failing in school, getting into fights with classmates, stealing, and trying to cope with the fact that her parents had filed for divorce three months before. Jessica was crying out for help long before she came to the attention of the emergency department of the hospital in her community. Both her parents cared about her, but they never really sensed the depth of Jessica's inner turmoil. Neither did her teachers.

———

Many people think that childhood and adolescence are "the best years of your life," characterized by carefree living with no serious responsibilities to weigh you down. The reality can be very different. Kids today face pressures that sometimes overwhelm them, delaying their development and leaving them unable to reach their potential in later life. Their challenges may range from attention and learning problems to physical or sexual abuse, eating disorders, drug and alcohol abuse, depression, anxiety, and family discord — to name only a few.

Most people don't think of nine-year-old children as wanting to die. But even mild emotional problems, left untreated, can grow and reach into the teen and young adult years, significantly crippling anyone's ability to become the person God created them to be. Prevention, assessment, and counselling are all effective means for enabling tomorrow's generation to reach their full potential. The church plays an important role in all three of these areas; pastoral care for children and youth is an important Christian ministry [Cheryl Noble, *IFL Reflections*, Spring 1999, Institute of Family Living].

"For the good of the child"

A therapy centre such as the Institute of Family Living gets many referrals of children and adolescents from clergy, doctors, schools, social workers, and parents. My colleague Dr. Cheryl Noble, a clinical psychologist specializing in children and youth, describes her approach with Jessica and others.

The current emphasis on the best interest of the child greatly influences how I work with young clients. My approach to children and youth can be described as collaborative and problem-solving. Everyone has problems in life. However, like some adults, many young persons define their whole existence by their problem. They may describe themselves with a label such as ADHD [Attention Deficit Hyperactivity Disorder], "sad," "learning-disabled," "nervous," or even "a kid from a broken family" [Cheryl Noble, *IFL Reflections*, Spring 1999, Institute of Family Living].

A fifteen-year-old boy was referred for therapy for depression and underachievement in school. He told Cheryl, "There's no use talking to my school or my parents. What can they do?

I'm ADD and nobody is going to do anything anyway." This young person was defining himself by a diagnosis that, for him, became his identity. He neglected to say, however, that he wrote songs, or that he could play any musical instrument that he picked up, and his mother added that he could be very persuasive in his dealings with people. Cheryl worked together with him to re-frame his life story. By expanding on areas of his life that were already successful, he was eventually able to see that he was much more than just "ADD" or "broken."

Teachers may see a young person as capable of achieving well, but his or her performance doesn't measure up. No two children learn identically. Some need the school curriculum adapted to meet their needs, and others need expectations (their own or those of the adults in their lives) adjusted to be more realistic. Sometimes young people don't see themselves as having a problem. They claim that their parents and school are the ones with the problem. When Cheryl asked an eight-year-old why her parents had brought her to see her, she stated, "There's nothing wrong with me. Everybody keeps bugging me." The task, as she saw it, was how to get everybody off her back. So together they explored actions she could take that might lead to this result.

Parents and teachers, youth leaders and coaches, are invaluable resources in helping a child acquire the skills he or she needs for long-term adaptation to life, as opposed to short-term Band-Aid solutions. Frequently, a problem-solving approach with young people involves teaching coping strategies to deal with similar issues that may arise in the future. While work with an individual is often indicated, equally often a young person's environment may need restructuring so that the problem does not perpetuate itself. For example, if a child becomes explosive during transitional times, the environment might be restructured to offset potential explosive behaviour [Cheryl Noble, *IFL Reflections,* Spring 1999, Institute of Family Living].

Children, family, and stress

This topic has been addressed in other chapters in this book, but it is important to emphasize that children do indeed experience stress and stress-related illnesses and emotional meltdowns. Because not everyone is created with the same hardwiring in the brain, some children feel overwhelmed more easily than do others. Here, accommodation may be the answer. One child may need more sleep than another, or may need to eat small frequent meals rather than the traditional three square meals a day, or may need to receive instructions one at a time. These small, achievable changes in a child's environment can reduce stress for the entire family.

Sometimes what we regard as abnormal behavioural or emotional expression is the most adaptive way that a child or youth can deal with an abnormal situation. Treating the child as if they were a label and nothing more is counter-productive. Working with a child of any age requires an integrative approach — involving the family and siblings, parents, grandparents, and friends, as well as the school system. The behaviour of children and youth needs to be seen in the context of the whole system in which they are involved — family, school, friendship networks, extracurricular activities, and church.

During times of profound stress in a child's life, a faith community can play a healing and restorative role by providing unconditional love and acceptance, however challenging this may be. As was mentioned in the case of the Smith-Lam family (in chapter 3), the son in prison was visited by his church's

From Parent to Child

I gave you life,
    but cannot live it for you.
I can teach you things,
    but I cannot make you learn.
I can give you directions,
    but I cannot be there to lead you.
I can allow you freedom,
    but I cannot account for it.
I can take you to church,
    but I cannot make you believe.
I can teach you right from wrong,
    but I cannot always decide for you.
I can buy you beautiful clothes,
but I cannot make you beautiful inside.

I can offer you advice,
    but I cannot accept it for you.
I can give you love,
    but I cannot force it upon you.
I can teach you to share,
    but I cannot make you unselfish.
I can teach you to respect,
    but I cannot force you to show honour.
I can advise you about friends,
    but I cannot choose them for you.
I can warn you about drugs,
    but I can't prevent you from using them.
I can tell you about lofty goals,
    but I cannot achieve them for you.
I can teach you about kindness,
    but I cannot force you to be gracious.
I can warn you about sins,
    but I cannot make your morals.
I can pray for you,
    but I cannot make you walk with God.
            — *Anonymous*

youth leader, who played a critical role in the youth's subsequent probation and significant life changes, which included accepting his newly reconfigured family system.

Positive parenting

There have been many how-to books written about parenting. Some stress the authority of the parent; others stress the needs of children. One author who has sought to find a balance between these sometimes competing demands is Barbara Coloroso. In her 1994 book *Kids Are Worth It!* she outlines six critical life messages inherent in good parenting:

- I trust you.
- I believe in you.
- I know you can handle this.
- You are listened to.
- You are cared for.
- You are very important to me.

The importance of emotional attachment and social integration are acknowledged in these six life messages. The relationship of the child to himself or herself (and thus the need for learning autonomy), and the relationship of the child to another (and thus the need for love, trust, and belonging) are foundational to emotional and interpersonal health. For optimal development, children need bonds of attachment with a warm and caring parent figure, clear and consistent household structure, timely comforting in a responsive environment, and the stimulation of language and thinking.

We now know that children have various ways of exploring and relating to the world. Whether they are "smart" in the area of nature, words, numbers, pictures, music, body, other people, or themselves, children have different gifts, and it is the responsibility of the adults in their lives to call forth these gifts. The work of Dr. Howard Gardiner at Harvard University's Graduate School of Education's "Project Zero" shows that all these "multiple intelligences" need to be nurtured and encouraged.

Thomas Armstrong elaborates on the work of Gardiner and helps parents, teachers, child care and youth workers to explore the multiple intelligences of children with whom they are involved. He encourages adults to develop a list of simple activities that involve a child's different intelligences — for example, make up a story (word smart), do a math problem (number smart), draw a horse (picture smart), sing a song (music smart), do a cartwheel (body smart), share something you really like about yourself (self smart), tell a friend something you really like about him or her (people smart), find a bird outside and watch where it flies (nature smart) [Thomas Armstrong, *In Their Own Way*, p. 227].

Jesus paid a great deal of attention to children, and the gospels are full of instances of Jesus relating to children, or citing them as role models. In the gospel of Luke, for example, there are several instances of Jesus healing children of parents who sought his help (the widow's son at Nain, Luke 7:11–17; the daughter of Jairus, Luke 8:40–56; a man's epileptic son, Luke 9:37–43), and he points to a child to illustrate the reign of God to his disciples who were jostling for preferential position.

An argument arose among them as to which one of them was the greatest. But Jesus, aware of their inner thoughts, took a little child and put it by his side, and said to them, "Whoever welcomes this child in my name welcomes me, and whoever welcomes me welcomes the one who sent me; for the least among all of you is the greatest" [Luke 9:46–48].

Raising children is a community task that requires the resources of parents, grandparents, godparents, aunts and uncles, teachers, youth workers, coaches, and neighbours. Occasionally, counsellors and therapists are needed to help for a time also. We are all called to welcome the child and to practise generous hospitality to the children who cross our path.

Here is an exercise to help us think about our own childhood and the children now in our lives:

- *Think of the significant people in your childhood.*
  Who helped you to experience a sense of joy?
  Who helped you to know yourself and value yourself?
  Who affirmed your gifts and talents?
- *Think of the number of roles you now play in various children's lives.*
  What gives you the greatest joy as you engage in their lives?
  How do you help them to come to accept themselves?

We need to give our children *roots* and *wings*. *Roots* to be grounded in relationship, in a solid sense of self, in religious faith, and in a worldview that will help them to stand strong in the face of trial and suffering. *Wings* to fly, to explore, to discover, to develop a sense of interdependence and an awareness of their unique giftedness. With both roots and wings, children can grow into a true capacity for interdependence, to be a "self in community." Here are some further questions we can ask ourselves about our relationship with the children in our lives.

- What are children telling you that you are resisting hearing?
- When are you most "present" to them, and not preoccupied or too busy to see and hear their needs?
- Do you allow them to ask for what they want, to find their

own "voice"? Or do they have to depend on you for permission to even ask?

- How do you give them the freedom to feel and to express their own feelings?
- Do you allow your children to take risks, to learn from their mistakes? Or do you teach them to "play safe" and perhaps then to fear failure?
- Do you open up, or shut down, children's natural curiosity and sense of adventure?

The societal picture

All of us who take the beautiful risk of loving and caring for children know that no one has all the right answers, and that we need help to encourage children to grow and mature into the people that God created them to be. So we are confronted with the dilemma of how to help children to remain faithful to God and to others, when all around them they see generations of broken relationships, either in their own or their friends' families, and a satiated society lacking in enduring connections.

In his paper entitled *40 Years of Evolution in Families* [May 2003], Robert Glossop, executive director of the Vanier Institute of the Family, described the scope of the changes that have occurred in family life over the last forty years. These changes have profoundly affected the lives of children in our society. As Glossop reports, citing Statistics Canada, there were ten times as many divorces in 2003 as in 1963. "And, of course, divorce rates now underestimate the number of conjugal dissolutions because you have to be married before you can get divorced. Here in Canada 16% of all couples are living common-law ... and in Quebec 29.8% of couples are living common-law."

In fact, 13% of children from birth to age fourteen are living with parents who are not married. "In comparison to forty years ago when well under 10% of children were born to unmarried mothers, 50% of children born in Quebec and 33% of those born in the other provinces are born to women who are not married." Glossop adds the significant fact that the majority of these newborns of unmarried parents go home from the hospital with both a mother and a father. Also he describes the common-law unions in Quebec as "being more stable over time than elsewhere."

The statistical record tells us that one in five Canadian children do not live with two parents and, of these, more than 80% live with a lone-parent mother. Further, 12% of all families are stepfamilies. Five out of ten include only the biological children of the mother. Four out of ten stepfamilies are blended and include children of two separate conjugal unions. Looking at the overall picture, we see that a relatively large percentage of children is going to experience the separation or divorce of their biological parents, perhaps as high as 40% to 45%. Most of these will live in a lone-parent family for a period of time. And most of these will experience an episode of poverty. Some will find themselves in a stepfamily home.

"Separation and divorce and all the changes they bring are hard on kids — terribly hard on kids. Most survive and do well. Some do not. None will be untouched by the experience. There are, indeed, long-term consequences in terms of their emotional health, academic achievement, and subsequent family relationships. If children could vote here, divorce might, as Judith Wallerstein once suggested, be illegal. [But it is encouraging that] the large majority of divorces in Canada are handled outside the courts and in fact parents are able to act in the best interests of their children" [Robert Glossop, *40 Years of Evolution in Families*].

The church and family reconfiguration

When we look at the essence of family life — the structure, function, and feelings — we see that children are profoundly affected in all three ways by the consumer culture of expressive individualism, whose values of impermanence are implicitly taught to children. Teens are exposed to pornography on the Internet, to consumer dating on shows such as *Bachelor*, to music videos that promote the consumption of sex, relationships, and things.

Into this cultural context our faith speaks a word of hope and consistency — that God is love, that forgiveness and mercy are foundational values in the journey of following Christ, and that community is to be treasured. Parenting is a calling from God; children are a gift. This message must be communicated to our children as they face the dislocations of family breakup and parental separations. Too often they feel caught in the middle, or are vulnerable to self-rejection or to feeling responsible for their parents (role reversal).

When new parental unions and family reconfigurations occur, the church can be a supportive community, as children and youth face the daunting prospect of including a new stepparent into their family circle, and often the addition of stepsiblings. Certainly trust and friendship do not happen instantly but must be carefully cultivated. Again, the community of the church can be a safe place, and a trusted youth leader can be a major support in listening to the confusion and hurts and fears of a young person going through such a major transition.

Parents in successful stepfamilies have realistic expectations and are comfortable in knowing that their stepfamily will always be different from a biological family unit. Both parents and children feel more comfortable when they recognize that not all relationships are equally close. Research on stepfamilies

The Blended Family Life Cycle

Stage: End of previous partnership
- Establishing emotional closure; grieving the losses.
- Examining patterns of family of origin and previous relationships.
- Beginning the children's emotional separation from unified parental system; reconfiguring parental custody/access.

Stage: Courtship
- "Dating"; learning to trust again in an intimate relationship. Children growing to know new partner (and his/her children).
- Establishing clear boundaries of who is in authority roles; children maintaining old loyalties while establishing new ties.

Stage: Getting married
- Establishing an intimate living relationship with a spouse. Further development of the emotional patterns of children relating to first parent while establishing new relationship(s) with parent's partner in home(s).

Stage: Parenting
- Opening the family to include new members; possible birth of new child(ren) to couple.
- Children coming and going from family unit.
- Negotiating the parenting roles.

Stage: Living with adolescents
- Increasing the flexibility of the family boundaries to allow the adolescent(s) to move in and out of the family system.

Stage: Launching children; "empty nest" phase
- Accepting the multitude of exits from, and new entries into, the family system.
- Adjusting to the ending of parenting roles.

Stage: Retirement
- Adjusting to the ending of wage-earning roles. Developing new relationships with adult children, their partners, grandchildren, and each other.

Stage: Old age
- Dealing with lessening abilities and greater dependence on others, and with losses of friends, family members, and eventually each other.

Adapted by Diane Marshall from Ed Bader, "Working with Families," *Australian Family Physician,* April 1990.

tells us that the quality of the step-parent/stepchild relationship is an important determinant of overall stepfamily happiness. Because the solid foundation of early childhood bonding experiences is lacking, the step-parent/stepchild bond may be particularly vulnerable to family stress.

Stepfamily research suggests that both husbands and wives generally feel closer to their own children than they do to their stepchildren. So in times of stress, parents are much more likely to side with their own children, and in turn, their children tend to reciprocate by showing appreciation and affection toward them, thereby distancing the step-parent. Because stepchildren and step-parents do not have the same history, a "more deliberate effort from both parties may be required to build and maintain a congenial relationship" [Melody Preece, "When Lone Parents Marry," *Transitions,* Winter 2003–2004].

Because stepfamilies are becoming more common, our churches need to look at positive ways to support and foster family life amid the complexities of modern culture. Marriage preparation is different for first-time marrying couples than it is for remarrying couples. In the latter case, professional or informal counselling that explores the previous marital history, custody and access issues around children, and personal learnings through the breakup, may be an important prerequisite to the new marriage.

And because communication skills, so needed in family life, may be more acute in stepfamily situations, a church designing its education program would do well to consider groups for stepparents separate from those for parents of intact families. Clergy, Sunday school teachers, and youth workers do well to be aware of the complexities of families with whom they work, and the specific needs of children and youth they serve.

Churches also need to be very sensitive to the realities of sole-parent families. Not only are such families likely to have had a major adjustment in their income and possibly a loss of the family home; but also most frequently, as Statistics Canada figures show, they are mother-led families bereft of fathers and of healthy male influence in the lives of their children. Programs that include child care or financial help for babysitting costs enable single mothers to participate in church life and to experience the encouragement and friendship that help to sustain them in their often lonely and difficult task of parenting their children.

Too often sole mothers do not get breaks from work and family, because of the lack of trustworthy childcare and adequate financial resources to afford it. Children in such homes do not receive the valuable input of others in their upbringing. "Adoptive" grandparents or "big brothers" can go a long way toward enriching the life of a child or youth who is living in a mother-led family.

Children, youth, and violence

In 2003, Family Service Canada and the Canadian Council on Social Development together conducted the first-ever national study to probe parental perceptions about the many forms of violence their children encounter. Over one thousand parents were surveyed, and focus groups were staged across the country. The results were summarized in a report entitled *Canadian Children's Exposure to Violence: What it Means for Parents.*

The study revealed that children are growing up in a world different from their parents, and that many parents have not grasped the scope of the problem. "They do not seem to recognize that their kids face a steady onslaught of aggressive images and incidents rather than simply isolated incidents; nor did parents seem to realize that the barrage of violence might have cumulative effects on their children," suggests Judi Varga-Toth, national programs manager at Family Service Canada.

Studies on children's exposure to violence indicate that television, videos, movies and aggression at school (including bullying) can negatively affect their development in the short and the long term. The vast majority of parents in the study expressed some concern about their children's exposure to violence at school and through entertainment media such as television and music videos, and more than 50% also expressed some concern about violence in the community. But only 30% voiced concern about sibling aggression, which has been described as the most common form of family violence.

Despite highly publicized cases of so-called rink rage,

where parents have assaulted or shouted obscenities at minor hockey officials, only 51% of parents expressed any concern about sport violence. In the focus groups, parents again cited the schoolyard and television as their primary concerns [*Let's Talk Families*, vol. 14, no. 3, October 2003].

Paul Roberts, a co-author of the national study, noted that some parents feel "almost helpless." This underscores one purpose of the study, which is to get parents to understand, and to seek to minimize the impact of, the aggression bombarding their children. One important step is for parents to discard their assumption that bullying is a normal part of growing up. Valuable resources — such as the Internet site www.bullying.org — are available to parents and teachers; and it is encouraging that many schools are actively developing effective anti-bullying programs, with the cooperation of parents.

Bill Belsey, founder of the bullying web site, notes that parents frequently send mixed signals to children about aggression, rationalizing that the media create an appetite for violence but that they are powerless to control their children's media habits. Many parents have no rules about what or how much television may be watched by their children. Studies have shown that more than 33% of parents use the TV rating system to help choose what programs their children may watch, but that only 36% of parents had installed filters on their Internet system

The co-authors of the recent study on parental attitudes to violence realized that a large proportion of parents do not feel comfortable with the role of censoring what their kids are exposed to. Nor do parents take a close enough look at the pressures associated with sports, which often produce aggressive behaviour in children.

It is commendable, in this regard, that the Canadian Hockey Association has started placing greater emphasis on parent education, and has taken steps to protect children through its "Speak Out" harassment and abuse prevention program. Speak Out encourages children to confide in a trusted adult whenever they feel uncomfortable about a situation, and requires coaches to attend a workshop offering them clear guidelines about not only how to react to disclosures of abuse or harassment, but also how to prevent it.

For the groups behind the *Canadian Children's Exposure to Violence* study, the primary goal is to help Canadian parents recognize just how much violence their children encounter daily, and to challenge parental ignorance about the effects of desensitizing children to aggression, which then places them at risk for bullying or being bullied.

Assertive versus aggressive communication

Consider three basic interpersonal styles — aggressive, passive, and assertive.

- People who use the *aggressive* style of interacting attempt to get their own way through intimidation, with little concern for how the other person might be feeling. The advantage of this style is that you feel in control and won't be pushed around.
- People who use the *passive* style of interacting tend to let other people push them around, do not stand up for themselves, and can be coerced to behave in certain ways even when they disagree. The advantage of this style is that you feel you won't be rejected.
- People who use the *assertive* style of interacting are able to express their feelings and wishes directly and openly while still respecting the other. The advantage of this style is that

you won't be pushed around and you won't push others around, and a deeper understanding will result.

Children need to be taught the skills of assertive communication. As parents, grandparents, teachers, or youth leaders we can make inquiries that will help children and adolescents to understand themselves and then to communicate assertively. This might include open-ended questions such as:

- What do you want?
- What do you need right now?
- How do you feel about this?
- What bothers you?
- What is the problem?

Helping children to recognize their own needs, make them known, and express them clearly is a challenging task. It helps when adults can guide children to stick to *one issue at a time* and to request *small changes* that do not overwhelm the child and lead to discouragement. Using what we call *"I" statements* ("I feel hurt"), rather than *"you" statements* ("you are thoughtless"), allows a child or young person to hear another's feelings without being blamed in humiliating or shaming ways.

Ultimately, assertive communication in families improves the problem solving abilities of the family members and also builds a climate of cooperation and mutual understanding. Assertiveness is a method of communication that is based on, and values, respect and equality. It does not undermine parental authority, but it does empower people of all ages to hear one another and to respond to one another more empathically. It is a practical part of the living out of Paul's teaching in Ephesians 4:15, which instructs us to "speak truthfully in love," and in Colossians 3:15, which encourages us to "let the peace of Christ rule in our hearts."

Encouragement: Building another person's confidence and feelings of self-worth

- Encouragement is the process of *focusing on the assets and strengths* of other people in order to build their self-confidence and feelings of worth.
- Focus on what is good about the person or the situation. *See the positive.*
- Seek to accept people *as they are.* Don't make your love and acceptance dependent on their behaviour.
- *Respect others.* It will reinforce their self-respect.
- Let others know their worth. *Recognize improvement and effort,* not just accomplishment.
- *Give encouragement* for effort or improvement. It implies a spirit of cooperation.
- Reserve praise for outstanding accomplishment. It implies a spirit of competition.
- One of the most powerful forces in human relationships is expectations. We can influence a person's behaviour by *changing our expectations* of the person.
- Lack of faith in both adults and children helps them to *anticipate failure.*
- Standards that are too high invite failure and discouragement.
- Avoid using discouraging words and actions.
- Avoid tacking qualifiers to your words of encouragement. Don't give with one hand and take away with the other.
- The sounds of encouragement are *words that build feelings of adequacy:*
  - I like the way you handled that.
  - I know you can handle it.
  - I appreciate what you did.
  - It looks as if you worked very hard on that.
  - You're improving.
- Avoid competition; *focus on cooperation.*
- Be *generous* with your encouragement.

How the church can help

One of the most effective ways church communities can help parents, grandparents, children, and youth is to sponsor workshops on conflict resolution stressing non-violent ways of dealing with conflict. Church youth groups could address directly the issues of aggression in the media, and sponsor panels and discussions on topics such as sex and dating, music videos, sports, or the effect of violence in our culture. Such dialogue can help young people understand and become more aware of possessing or condoning attitudes and behaviours that violate others.

Training in non-violence is foundational to living out our Christian calling to be peacemakers. Church-sponsored parenting groups, lectures, and workshops can encourage parents to develop skills to be non-violent in the way they exercise authority. Frequently, parents are judged to be "bad" by their fellow churchgoers if they provide a lack of supervision, discipline, or affection, but seldom does the church address the bigger issue of parents' lack of time. Many Christian parents struggle with coordinating a work/family balance without adequate supports or effective tools to actually *be* parents. Community church-based programs that help beleaguered parents develop the necessary skills can go a long way to reduce family violence and to improve parent-child relationships.

Resources

Parenting

Armstrong, Thomas, Ph.D. 2000. *In Their Own Way: Discovering and Encouraging Your Child's Multiple Intelligences.* New York: Jeremy Tarcher/ Putnam.

Coloroso, Barbara. 1994. *Kids Are Worth It — Giving Your Child the Gift of Inner Discipline.* Toronto: Somerville House.

____. 1999. *Parenting with Wit and Wisdom in Times of Chaos and Loss.* New York: Penguin Books.

____. 2002. *The Bully, the Bullied and the Bystander.* 2002. New York: HarperCollins.

Hendrix, Harville, and Helen Hunt. 1997. *Giving the Love that Heals: A Guide for Parents.* New York: Atria Books.

Wolf, Anthony. 1991. *Get Out of My Life But First Could You Drive Me and Cheryl to the Mall? A Parent's Guide to the New Teenager.* Toronto: Harper Collins.

Welcome to Parenting Video. 1997. A five-part series on parenting and healthy child development, from birth to six years. Available from Family Service Canada for $17.99. Telephone 613-722-9006. Internet: <info@familyservicecanada.org>.

KidsProtect. A service of MedicAlert, this program offers a customized medical identification bracelet or necklet for your child with a 24-hour emergency hotline linked to their medical and personal records, immediately accessible to health care professionals in all emergencies. Also available for low-income families through the KidsProtect Assistance program. For more information, call 1-800-668-1507, or check out <www.kidsprotect.ca>.

Parent-Child

Mundy, Michaelene. 1999. *Mad Isn't Bad: A Child's Book about Anger.* Elf-Help Book for Kids. One Caring Place, St. Meinrod, Indiana: Abbey Press.

Wigand, Molly. 2000. *Help Is Here for Facing Fear.* Elf-Help Book for Kids. One Caring Place, St. Meinrod, Indiana: Abbey Press.

Divorce, Remarriage, and the Family

Flach, Frederic. 1998. *A New Marriage, a New Life: Making Your Second Marriage a Success.* New York: Hatherleigh Press.

Mosely, Doug, and Naomi Moseley. 1998. *Making your Second Marriage a First-Class Success.* Rocklin, CA: Prime Publishing

Thomas, Christine. 1999. *Second Wives: The Silent Struggle.* Monarch Books.

Wallerstein, Judith S., Julia M. Lewis, and Sandra Blakeslee. 2000. *The Unexpected Legacy of Divorce: A 25 Year Landmark Study.* New York: Hyperion.

Journals, Reports, and Papers

Canadian Children's Exposure to Violence: What it Means for Parents. The summary of this report can be obtained by consulting the Canadian Council on Social Development (CCSD). Internet <www.ccsd.ca>.

Glossop, Robert, Ph.D. 2003. *40 Years of Evolution in Families.* Paper presented to the 40th Anniversary Conference of the Association of Family and Conciliation Courts, Ottawa, 28 May.

____ ."Demographics, Family Law and Money." 2003. Plenary address to the Family Law Seminar of the National Judicial Institute, Vancouver, 12 February.

Noble, Cheryl, Ph.D. Spring 1999. "For the Good of the Child." *IFL Reflections.* Toronto: Institute of Family Living.

Transition. Vanier Institute on the Family. Winter 2003–2004, vol. 33, no. 4. Three articles from this journal, including Heather Juby, "Yours, Mine, and Ours: New Boundaries for the Modern Stepfamily"; Melody Preece, "When Lone Parents Marry: The Challenge of Stepfamily Relationships"; and Patricia Kelley, "Suddenly Siblings: Helping Children Adapt to Life in a Stepfamily."

Let's Talk Families. Family Service Canada. October 2003, vol. 14, no. 3. An article in this report, Brenda Branswell, "Young Again: Helping Parents See the Realities of Youth Exposure to Violence."

Time Magazine. 25 September 2000. "What Divorce Does to Kids." Feature issue.

6
Addiction and Recovery

> As long as we are still wrestling with the problems of
> desire and gratification, the world will be perceived
> as not meeting our desire. If it doesn't have to "satisfy"
> us, then the more free we are to find the material world
> a gift. The more our desire is for God, the more we
> can allow the stuff of the world to be what it is as gift.
>
> — A Ray of Darkness, *Rowan Williams,*
> *Archbishop of Canterbury*

Referred by his pastor, Thomas entered counselling after his wife discovered him viewing pornography on the Internet. Understandably he was embarrassed and felt a great deal of shame in talking with both his priest and his wife. His compulsive use of pornography had been with him since his teenage years. He was a shy man, not accustomed to sharing his feelings openly, and it was a challenge for him to work with a therapist. Through therapy he was able to look at his pattern of managing stress and avoiding his feelings, and to take seriously his compulsive use of pornography. He began to see how it distanced him from his wife and from a healthy sexual relationship in their marriage.

Jennie was a bright teenager whose marks became increasingly poor as she missed her morning classes and failed to complete her homework assignments. At fourteen she wore baggy clothes, was obsessed with her body image, and counted every calorie. She argued with her siblings and parents about their weight, and refused to come to the dinner table for meals, insisting on eating alone in the kitchen on her own time, or in her room. One day her older sister found her vomiting in the bathroom and confronted her about being bulimic. Together with their mother, her sister persuaded Jennie to seek the help of a therapist. It was a long journey over many months, but Jennie slowly began to accept her body and to become aware of the "beauty culture" and its effect on women and girls.

Margaret was a member of her church choir. After several weeks of smelling alcohol on her breath and finding her hostile and non-cooperative in choir practice, the choir director became concerned and spoke to their minister. Aware that Margaret had been widowed a year earlier, the minister wasn't sure how to confront the situation. She spoke to a therapist to whom she regularly referred members of her congregation, and was encouraged to engage the help of Margaret's adult daughter in an intervention process. During this process it became obvious that Margaret was drinking alone most nights, and not eating well. The minister made contact with a treatment centre and helped to facilitate an intervention. Margaret became an outpatient and eventually entered a treatment program. Her daughter, a university student, joined Al-Anon and was given help to effectively deal with her mother's recovery.

How do addictions develop?

The addiction process in our culture appears to have both psychological and behavioural dimensions. It affects the way we think and feel and act. All addictions hold some characteristics in common and other characteristics specific to the particular addiction. An essential component of any addiction is that it keeps us out of touch with our inner selves — our feelings, morality, and awareness. There are several recognized addictive processes:

- drug addiction and alcoholism;
- eating disorders;
- smoking;
- sexual addictions (including Internet pornography) ;
- compulsive spending;
- gambling;
- shoplifting;
- workaholism; and
- rage.

All of these processes lead people to develop certain ritualistic behaviours and thought patterns that may have devastating effects on interpersonal relationships. Although there are many kinds of addiction, every addicted person engages in a relationship with an *object* (which may include a substance) or an *event,* in order to produce a desired mood change. Those who treat addictions frequently find that there are common underlying causes such as mood disorders and un-grieved grief. For example, men who are addictively violent and have rages are often suffering from untreated depression [Terence Real, *I Don't Want to Talk About It: Overcoming the Secret Legacy of Male Depression*].

Within the *chemical dependency* field, an addiction is broadly considered to be the compulsive need for any substance outside the person. An addiction to an addictive substance, such as food or chemicals (alcohol and drugs), is often called an "ingestive addiction."

By comparison, an addiction to a way of living (which sometimes leads to an ingestive addiction) is called a "process addiction." For example, the "dry drunk" is a person who exhibits the behaviours, attitudes, and thinking associated with the active disease of alcoholism, but does not actually use the chemical any longer. Such a person acts is if he or she is using the ingestive agent, even though not doing so. In this case not drinking does not constitute recovery.

For a person addicted to alcohol to become sober and maintain sobriety, she or he has to make major changes in lifestyle. This is true for the alcoholic and the drug and food addict as well. The Twelve Step program of Alcoholics Anonymous (AA) is a set of tools designed not only to help an addicted person move away from substance abuse, but also to bring about a change from the addictive process to healthy habits of thinking and living. The Twelve Steps are adaptable to any addiction, whether process or ingestive.

A Culture of Addiction

Our culture has been described as an addictive culture. Subway advertisements bombard us with pictures of ultra-thin semi-naked women as we rush to work; television commercials proclaim the wonders of beer and the "good life" that comes from drinking with one's buddies; lottery tickets and casinos encourage us to gamble as a normal part of life; and music videos confront teenagers with compelling images of sex, violence, and drugs. It has been estimated that a high percentage of all helping professionals (including clergy) are not themselves aware of factors leading to addiction, and hence at many levels, perpetuate and enable the addictive *process*. In addition, many professionals are themselves addicts — including the addiction of being workaholics.

There can be a complex overlapping of addictions and mental illness in families. Many addictions have an underlying cause in mood disorders, which may mask anxiety or depression or some other psychiatric condition that needs treatment. Conversely, symptoms of depression or manic-depression (bipolar disorder) may arise from a family history of some readily identifiable chemical dependency. Frequently, to overcome the addiction, the underlying anxiety or depression must be treated.

People's emotional and intimacy needs are normally met through connections with other people, the community, themselves, or a spiritual power greater than themselves. However, addicted persons tend to form a substitute "relationship" with the addictive process or substance. There are many theories of why addictions develop. According to Craig Nakken (an addictionologist), addiction is a "pathological love and trust relationship with an object/substance or event" [Craig Nakken, *The Addictive Personality*, pp. 10–11].

So whenever a person acts in addictive ways, their behaviour forces them to withdraw, to become internally preoccupied, and to isolate themselves from others. The longer an addictive process progresses, the less a person feels the ability to have meaningful relationships with others. This further perpetuates the experience of loneliness and isolation, and may lead to further acting out — that is, engaging in more addictive behaviour.

When pain creates an emotional need, an addict may turn to their specific addiction for relief, just as a non-addict may turn to a spouse, to a close friend, or to spiritual nourishment. Addicts learn to trust their addictively-created mood change because it is consistent and predictable. In its beginning stages the addiction process develops as an attempt to emotionally fulfill oneself, yet its long-term effect is to emotionally numb and to eventually deaden the self. As Nakken says, "Addicts trust they will experience a mood change if they perform certain behaviours.... And although finding emotional fulfillment through an object or event is an illusion, it is an illusion that ... helps to counteract the total sense of powerlessness and unmanageability the addict is feeling on a deeper, more personal level" [Nakken, p. 14].

And so, addicted people may confuse the intensity of acting out their addiction with a kind of intimacy. Because they feel connected to the moment of intensity, they believe it is a moment of intimacy. In fact, it is nurturance through avoidance. For the addict, different objects and events (eating, gambling, pornography, drinking, chemicals, etc.) all have in common the ability to produce a positive and pleasurable mood change that is fundamentally rooted in emotional isolation, not in true relational connection. For example, men who rage, while feeling the initial release of discharging anger, later feel the anguish of shame, remorse, and often separation from their partner as a consequence of their pattern of violence.

The abuse cycle

The process of addiction involves movement, development, and change. As an addiction develops, it becomes a way of life, a life cycle. The diagram below illustrates this.

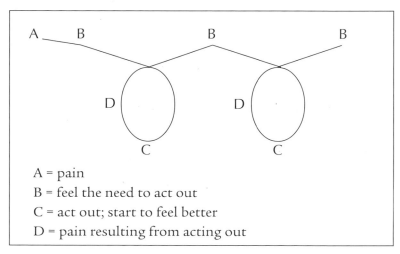

A = pain
B = feel the need to act out
C = act out; start to feel better
D = pain resulting from acting out

This cycle causes an emotional craving, resulting in a mental preoccupation, leading to a behavioural action, which leads back to the emotional hunger. For an addicted person, the feeling of discomfort becomes a signal to act out, not a signal to connect with others, with oneself, or with God.

The more a person seeks relief from inner emptiness and pain through addiction, the more *shame* they experience. As a result, they become shame-bound and lose self-respect, self-confidence, self-discipline, and self-love [John Bradshaw, *Healing the Shame that Binds You*]. The tragedy and ultimate lie of the addictive process is seen in the abuse cycle of the addict who, in seeking refuge from the pain of addiction, in fact moves further into the addictive process. "As the illness progresses, the delusional system will become more complex and have a quality of rigidity. The delusional system [of the addict] is commonly described as a wall surrounding the person" [Nakken, p. 34].

Rituals have been described as a language of behaviour, designed to give comfort at times of crisis or during times of conflict or stress. Religious worship uses ritual language and symbolism to express and evoke our relationship to God. But addicts use rituals and addictive rites to create a mood, to ease their tension or discomfort, and to produce a sense of release. The ritual of addiction has been described as an inner struggle between control and release; this struggle is characteristic of a person involved in an addictive process. And so, another way of describing the addictive cycle is as follows.

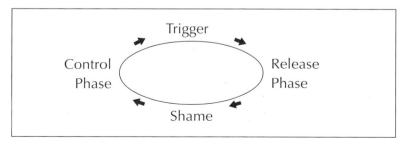

How can family members and churches help?

The family and the faith community both need to respond to the addicted person with a hope for healing. Historically the church has "walked by on the other side of the road" [Luke 10:25–37] from ignorance of the nature of addiction. Families have unwittingly enabled the addict by their failure to set limits, by denying and excusing and covering up for the addict's behaviour, and by increasing their own work load to compensate.

Since the mid-twentieth century, in the Twelve Step programs of AA and other groups, we've seen the concrete application of spiritual principles in the context of community. Such groups have become a fellowship of people in recovery — sharing instead of preaching, and calling forth the image of God in one another. John Bradshaw writes that, in his recovery from alcohol addiction, "the only way out of the shame (was) to embrace it.... When I came out of hiding, I discovered people who loved me for being just another stumbling human being" [John Bradshaw, "Our Families, Our Selves: The Shame of Toxic Shame," *Psychology Today,* July 1989].

For some people, defining addictive behaviour as a moral issue enables them to stop "cold turkey." For others, defining the addiction in terms of "morality" compounds the cycle of shame. The experience of withdrawal, of giving up the addictive substance or process, creates a big hole, an emptiness, which may have precipitated the numbing behaviour in the first place. If the addictive process is itself rooted in a compulsive acting out from feelings of emptiness, then the recovery process must help the addicted person to fill the emptiness in new ways that nurture the self. Moral proscriptions and judgemental attitudes on the part of family or friends will not encourage the addict to find life-affirming ways of behaving.

But unless a true recovery process is entered into, the addict may go from one addiction to another. For example, a compulsive smoker who stops smoking may develop an eating disorder. An alcoholic who stops drinking may develop a dependency on tranquilizers. Recovery is only truly possible if there is a rebuilding of the true self — the self made in the image of God. Frequently the addicted person has learned in childhood the survival strategy of disconnecting from his or her feelings as a means of adapting to a painful emotional reality. As a result, they feel an emotional emptiness that cries out to be filled. Their process of trying to fill the void becomes the addiction.

Because the addiction has served to disassociate the addict from his or her spiritual core, from the human journey of seeking integration between an event, a feeling, and the appropriate expression, it is not uncommon to hear someone in recovery say, "It took me two years in recovery before I could cry or even know I *could* cry," or "It took me two years to laugh!"

Thomas, Jennie, and Margaret all had supportive families and faith communities to help them in their healing journey. Overcoming addictive behaviours, thoughts, and processes took a combination of expert help, a support group, and the courageous commitment of each of these persons in their own

---

O blessed Jesus, you ministered to all who came to you. Look with compassion upon all who through addiction have lost their health and freedom. Restore to them the assurance of your unfailing mercy; remove the fears that attack them; strengthen them in the work of their recovery; and to those who care for them, give patient understanding and persevering love; for your mercy's sake [*Occasional Prayers, For Those Suffering from Addiction,* Book of Alternative Services, *p. 682*].

recovery. The presence of loving family and friends contributed to their healing, and prayerfully supported the faltering steps of rebuilding, nurturing the fruits of love and patience and honest communication in all persons involved.

Suggestions for families

Addiction contributes to family disintegration, but families can begin their recovery process with or without the participation of the practising addict. When addiction in a parent develops, the children do not have the firm relational tie that provides them with the security to explore their world safely. Addicted persons are often erratic and inconsistent, and children learn that it is not safe to talk about problems in the family. Where a child or spouse is in danger from the addict's behaviour, separation is frequently important.

But if there is not a dangerous situation and the addict still wants to participate in the family, family members can learn to relate in healthier non-co-dependent ways, which do not accommodate the addiction. Family members can learn to share feelings and needs with each other honestly, and to take responsibility for their own happiness and life direction without blaming the addict, hiding, or becoming trapped in shame.

Families can seek the help of a professional. Family physicians are frequently trained to help effect an intervention in the life of the addict, since many addictions are life and health threatening. Family therapists and addiction therapists are also trained professionals who can facilitate the help needed for the family members, even if the addict refuses to seek healing.

Twelve Step groups exist in cities and towns across Canada. Meetings are free and confidentiality is guaranteed through the principle of anonymity. There are Twelve Step recovery programs for the spouse and family members of the addict, as well as for the addict. In the Twelve Steps format, there is no judgement or condemnation. There are "sponsors" who will listen, who can help you cope, and will encourage you in making wise decisions.

Some strategies for coping with addictions

Here are some concrete steps families and churches can take to respond to addictions:

- Become informed: read books; visit open AA meetings.
- Seek professional help: clarify that you want someone trained in addictions.
- Be willing to see yourself as involved in the recovery process: the whole family needs to be involved in healing, which may begin through an intervention process.
- Be willing to take action.
- Be realistically hopeful.

Resources

Addicts in Recovery. 1994. *The Twelve Steps: A Spiritual Journey (A Working Guide for Healing)*. San Diego: RPI Publishing, Inc.

Beattie, Melody. 1990. *The Language of Letting Go*. Center City, Minnesota: Hazelden.

Bradshaw, John. 1988. *Healing the Shame That Binds You*. Deerfield Beach, Florida: Healing Communications Inc.

May, Gerald, M.D. 1988. *Addiction and Grace*. San Francisco: Harper.

Nakken, Craig. 1996. *The Addictive Personality: Understanding the Addictive Process and Compulsive Behavior*. Center City, Minnesota: Hazelden.

Real, Terence. 1997. *I Don't Want to Talk About It: Overcoming the Secret Legacy of Male Depression*. New York: Fireside (Simon and Schuster).

Schaef, Anne Wilson. 1986. *Co-dependence: Misunderstood — Mistreated*. Minneapolis: Winston Press.

Wegscheider Cruse, Sharon. 1989. *Another Chance: Hope and Health for the Alcoholic Family*. Palo Alto, California: Science and Behaviour Books.

Whitfield, Charles, M.D. 1994. *My Recovery: A Personal Plan for Healing*. San Diego: RPI Publishing, Inc.

7
Healing the Wounds of Trauma

God heals the brokenhearted
and binds up their wounds.

— *Psalm 147:3*

What do you do when you are lost in the forest?
Wherever you are is called "here"....
Stand still: the forest knows where you are.
Let it find you.

— *Salish poem*

The priest was called an hour before midnight by a frantic mother in his congregation. He could hear the desperation in her voice. "Please come over. My son has hit his father and threatened his little brother. I am afraid to call the police." The priest knew that this family, new to the congregation, had recently arrived in Canada, having spent three years in a refugee camp after fleeing their war-torn country. In spite of the late hour, the priest decided to pay a pastoral visit. He found a distraught family — the teenaged son ashamed of his anger toward his father and little brother, the parents and younger child bewildered and frightened.

This family was traumatized by war and their experience as refugees, their status still undecided in the long process of refugee claims. But now their anger against external events was being acted out in the inner life of the family, and that was adding to the trauma. The teenage son had been humiliated and called racist names at school. His sense of powerlessness was overwhelming, and he did what many victims do — took out his rage on some-one less powerful than himself.

In the wake of larger societal traumas, linked to economic and political injustice and strife, this family was living out their fear and powerlessness. They felt trapped. Their new country was not the idyllic and peaceful refuge they had imagined. They were living in poverty, and for the first time in their lives they were experiencing racism. They turned for spiritual sustenance to someone they could trust, and were helped to heal by the intervention of a wise and caring priest.

Trauma is more common than we think

The horrors of the 2001 terrorist attacks in the United States shattered our Canadian sense of invulnerability as a society. We found ourselves questioning things we took for granted, even though many of them had little or nothing to do with September 11 — a safe border with the United States, freedom from terrorism in North America, secure workplaces, an economy that provides many of us with more than enough. Now these are no longer "givens." The questions we are asking as Christians are, How can we live faithfully in the new emerging reality? Where do we find the inner peace that transforms our lives from living in fear to living in hope?

Many Canadian professionals were caught in or near the World Trade Center at the time of the terrorist attacks. Their journey of healing has required perseverance and assistance. For these otherwise previously sheltered Canadians, the process of recovery was akin to that of the refugee family. Similar challenges face all people who endure trauma and have to rebuild their lives — those who have experienced sexual abuse, rape, family violence, severe accidents, homicide, and suicide.

One of the biggest challenges to healing from a personal or communal disaster is to relearn (or perhaps to learn for the first time) how to feel safe in the world, safe in relationships, safe in one's own bodily self. People who suffer from trauma need to find a secure place not only to explore the memories of the traumatic event, but also to begin to imagine, learn, and practise the skills needed to rebuild their lives. Knowing that one is profoundly accepted and loved by God can give the courage to enter a therapeutic journey of healing.

Professional therapists may play an important role in assisting the journey. Therapists trained in trauma-focused therapy employ a variety of techniques that assist healing; medical doctors may need to assess and diagnose depression and anxiety, which are part of post-traumatic stress disorder, and to treat with appropriate medication. But the sufferers themselves, and their friends and supporters, are central to the healing process.

The challenge of healing from trauma is greater than simply restoring the neurotransmitters in the brain or reprocessing painful memories or learning new skills. Essentially, it is a spiritual process of finding hope and discovering once again the God-given capacity to be human — to love, trust, and laugh; to enjoy the beauties of divine and human creation; to experience community. Some of these approaches are detailed later in this chapter.

Spanking and physical punishment

Recently, CTV news aired the report of a panel of pediatricians and child care advocates entitled *The Joint Statement on Physical Punishment of Children and Youth*. The statement was endorsed by 138 Canadian organizations, including the Canadian Paediatric

Society, the Canadian Public Health Association, and Family Services Canada. The report comes out unequivocally against spankings, and calls for a ban on corporal punishment [CTV.ca News, 9 September 2004].

The study concludes that physical discipline is ethically wrong, doesn't work, and harms children. The authors report:

> The evidence is clear and compelling: Physical punishment of children and youth plays no useful role in their upbringing and poses only risks to their development. The research says spanking can harm children through:
> * physical injury;
> * depression, unhappiness, anxiety and feelings of hopelessness;
> * impaired empathy and moral judgement;
> * damaged relationships with parents;
> * antisocial behaviour; and
> * tolerance of violence in adulthood.

Physical punishment — defined as spanking, slapping, shaking, and biting — also includes such acts as washing a child's mouth out with soap, putting them in a confined space (a cupboard, for example), and denying them basic necessities (refusing to allow them food or drink or not allowing them to go to the bathroom).

Experts agree that children need limits, and that parents need to make decisions about their children's welfare. But instead of physical punishment they suggest proposing clear consequences, and setting clear limits (examples might be removing a child from the scene if she or he is hitting a sibling; establishing a rule that there will be no recreation until homework is done). They encourage parents to respect their children, talk with them, explain problems, and teach them alternative behaviours.

The joint statement goes on to say that "children in Canada must be given the same protection from physical assault as that given to Canadian adults." The researchers found that few parents believe that physical punishment is effective, but that those who did choose to use it were more likely to feel anger in response to their children's behaviour, to have experienced physical punishment themselves as children, to be subject to depression, or to be suffering undue stress.

What is post-traumatic stress disorder (PTSD)?

Historically, symptoms associated with what we now call PTSD were described back in ancient Greece. In the last century, soldiers from World War I and II were frequently diagnosed with "combat stress" or "shell shock." Many of us have heard family stories describing someone who returned from the war "a different person."

Similar reactions afflict people in situations that, at least from the outside, seem to be far less stressful than war. Since 1980, the revisions of the Diagnostic and Statistical Manual of Mental Disorders (DSM III and DSM IV) have recognized the interconnection of various trauma-related conditions. The field of traumatology is concerned with the systemic (interpersonal and intrarelational) causes and consequences of traumatic events.

Today, the diagnosis of PTSD is applied broadly to many emotional, behavioural, and identity reactions that follow such traumatic life experiences as accidents, natural disasters, acute illnesses, acts of terrorism, wartime stressors, physical, sexual, or psychological abuse. PTSD can also occur in persons who provide care to trauma victims, such as police officers, fire fighters, and health care personnel, including therapists and other mental health practitioners.

Many nurses and doctors suffered PTSD in the wake of the 2003 SARS (Severe Acute Respiratory Syndrome) emergency in Toronto hospitals, and Canadian peacekeeping troops have reported severe instances of PTSD when returning from Bosnia, Rwanda, and Afghanistan. General Romeo Dallaire made public his courageous stuggle with PTSD after returning from the horror of the Rwandan genocide.

One of the defining characteristics of PTSD is that a person continually re-experiences the traumatic event. Such memories cause the person to develop a wide range of symptoms — including trouble concentrating, distrust of others, angry outbursts, withdrawal, flashbacks, insomnia, nightmares, crying, sadness, dissociation, feelings of inadequacy or unworthiness, alienation from self, others, or work.

People who have experienced acute psychological trauma in the past often tend to respond to current stressors with emotions that have an intensity belonging to the past. Because intense fear is part of the felt experience of trauma, any current reminder of that fear creates acute anxiety. Thus, traumatized individuals may frequently rely on action (for example, sudden withdrawal or angry outbursts) rather than thought, when they feel threatened. This is of course bewildering, and can be deeply distressing to persons with whom they are in intimate relationships, whether as a couple or in a family context.

Christians often blame themselves, and others, for feelings of overwhelming fear. Some people tend to preach at, rather than empathize with, those in distress. Quoting scripture verses, such as "perfect love casts out fear," does not help; in fact, it may cause a trauma survivor to feel shame and guilt, further cutting them off from community. Simple acceptance, recognizing the dignity of the other, and patient understanding — all manifestations of the fruit of the Spirit — are what is required for healing and hope to be renewed.

Treatment of trauma

The professional treatment of trauma is usually divided into three stages — stabilization, trauma-focused therapy, and reconnecting with family, community, and friends. The role of a family therapist is to take seriously the place of the individual in their network of relationships and particularly the intimate connections of family. Family members and friends can be of great support to the healing process if they are helped to understand the symptoms and experience of their traumatized loved ones. Clergy and congregations can also help by providing a non-judgemental and caring community to help families heal.

When trust has been broken, children who have been sexually or physically abused need help in learning to respond to the genuine affection and warmth of a trustworthy family member. On the other hand, adults who have lived a long time with untreated childhood abuse may take years to learn how to build trusting intimate connections. They need to learn how to feel safe in interpersonal relationships, how to recognize and express feelings appropriately, how to relax, and how to think about deeply painful memories without becoming obsessed or shutting down emotionally. These abilities require the opportunity to process, grieve, and reclaim a sense of control over one's life, and to set realistic goals for one's future.

Often people who have experienced trauma — like the refugee family cited at the beginning of this chapter — can develop phobias, addictions, depression, psychosomatic illnesses, and increased interpersonal conflicts. For many, these conditions go away once the PTSD symptoms are treated appropriately with cognitive-behavioural therapy and anxiety management.

Therapy stabilized the refugee family's intense anxiety and facilitated the treatment for depression in the teenage son. It also, and most importantly, enabled them to work through the grief of all they had lost and the disappointment of all they had expected. Not only did they set more realistic goals as a family for their life in a new country; they found new ways to support and encourage each other, and to become part of their new church's community.

During the therapeutic process, they realized the need for more frequent communication and supportive interaction among themselves, and took steps to put in place such encouragement. Their priest became more sensitized to the nature of racism and the feelings that refugees can experience in being "strangers in a strange land," and he was able to more effectively preach and pray about the theme of hospitality. This then enabled the congregation to be more aware of the needs of newcomers in their midst.

The gift of hope

Hope is a gift of the Creator. Hope is necessary. Without it, who would dare to get out of bed in the morning? Yet when horrors such as the tsunami in Asia, or the events of September 11 happen, despair (the absence of hope) is an understandable first reaction. Have we human beings still not learned how to live in peace with ourselves and each other? After the events of September 11, playwright David Copelin wrote in the newsletter of the Institute of Family Living:

When we have hope, nothing can stop us. With hope, there's no guarantee of success. But hope helps us entertain the possibility that things just might turn out all right. Not because we lie around, passively waiting for that to happen, but because with hope we are liberated to do the necessary work, never accepting momentary setbacks as permanent. Terrorism terrifies, but only to the degree that we let it. Despair destroys, but hope brings life to life. As playwright Samuel Beckett put it, "I must go on. I can't go on. I'll go on."

The apostle Paul encourages us, in the Letter to the Philippians [4:8–10], to live one day at a time, sustained in the knowledge of God's love, and in the peace of Christ. He writes:

Finally, beloved, whatever is true, whatever is honourable, whatever is just, whatever is pure, whatever is pleasing, whatever is commendable, if there is any excellence and if there is anything worthy of praise, think about these things. Keep on doing the things that you have learned and received and heard and seen in me, and the God of peace will be with you.

Some strategies for coping with trauma and stressful circumstances

The following self-care strategies can help deal with the impact of traumatic stress.

What you can do for yourself

- Exercise regularly. Exercise alternated with relaxation will help alleviate physical reactions.

- Talk to people. Talk is healing; isolation is not. Accept support.
- Remember that loved ones, friends, colleagues, and neighbours care.
- Eat well-balanced, regular meals; drink in moderation. Be careful not to binge, eat junk food, or drink in excess to self-medicate.
- Don't make any big life changes immediately. During periods of extreme stress, we tend to have poor judgement.
- See your physician if you are having trouble sleeping or concentrating. Medication may help you manage depression and anxiety.

What family and friends can do for adults

- Listen and empathize. A sympathetic listener is very important.
- Spend time with the traumatized person. There is no substitute for personal presence.
- Offer assistance and sympathy. Voicing your support is crucial, as is giving permission for the traumatized person to ask for help.
- Don't lecture or tell the traumatized person to be stoical. Instead, tell the person who is suffering that you're sorry such an event has occurred and that you want to understand and support them.
- Respect a family member's need for privacy. People may need to grieve in private, as well as stay connected. Checking when someone needs space and time for privacy can be very supportive.

What family and friends can do to help children

The intense anxiety and fear that often follow a disaster or other traumatic event can be especially troubling for children, who often relive trauma through repetitive play, distressing daydreams, and nightmares. They may exhibit a variety of changes in their behaviours to which parents should pay attention.

Some may regress and demonstrate "younger" behaviours such as thumb-sucking or bed-wetting. Children may be more prone to nightmares and fear of sleeping alone. Performance in school may suffer. Other changes in behaviour patterns may include throwing tantrums more frequently or withdrawing and becoming more solitary. There are several things parents, teachers, and others who care for children, can do to help alleviate the emotional consequences of trauma, including the following:

- Be reassuring. Children need to feel emotionally protected and connected, so give them affection and a safe place to be comforted, always respecting children's boundaries.
- Model stability. Children take their cues from the ways their parents and other adults respond. Parents should admit their concerns to their children, but also show good coping strategies.
- Understand what a child can cope with. A child's reactions depend on how much destruction he or she sees during or after a disaster, and their age affects how they will respond. It is important to be careful about the television, movies, or computer information the child is exposed to, to make sure that what they see is age-appropriate, and to explain events in words the child can comprehend.

Resources

The Canadian Journal of CME (Continuing Medical Education). September 2001.

Figley, C., ed. 1988. *Burnout in Families: The Systemic Costs of Caring.* Boca Raton: CRC Press.

Herman, J. L. 1992. *Trauma and Recovery.* New York: Basic Books.

Matsakis, A. 1998. *Trust after Trauma: A Guide to Relationships for Survivors and Those Who Love Them.* Oakland, California: New Harbinger.

Sapolsky, R. M. 1998. *Why Zebras Don't Get Ulcers: An Updated Guide to Stress, Stress-Related Diseases, and Coping.* 2nd ed. New York: Freeman.

Schiraldi, G. R. 2000. *The Post-Traumatic Stress Disorder Sourcebook: A Guide to Healing, Recovery, and Growth.* Los Angeles: Lowell House.

Van der Kolk, B., A. C. McFarlane, and L. Weisath, eds. 1996. *Traumatic Stress: The Effects of Overwhelming Experience on Mind, Body, and Society.* New York: Guildford Press.

8
Spirituality and Healing

In communion with God ... Memory is transformed
into Hope; Understanding is transformed into Faith;
Will is transformed into Love.

— *St. John of the Cross*

The promise of God means the promise of every person
and every situation. The world is promising because God
has promised to be there. The faithfulness of God is ...
loving attention and responsiveness to the world he has
made.... Contemplation leads us to the reality of God,
whose being is in self-communicating.

— *A Ray of Darkness,* Rowan Williams,
Archbishop of Canterbury

A friend recently wrote me the following reflection:

I experienced a beautiful metaphor a few days ago. The city
was overshadowed by storm clouds in an arc over the sky,
and as I watched across the harbour, the sun spread from
the horizon, reflected on the underside of the dark clouds.
This created a mirage effect, bringing the outline of the
Niagara coast up clear, brightly lit and much closer than
usual. We need to believe that the Darkness can give opportunity for the Light to shine brighter and clearer than usual.

How often in families we are challenged by storm clouds, and need to hold to the promise and receive the vision that the light of God's love shines in the darkness and the darkness cannot put it out.

Commenting on such moments of awareness in her own life, Renita Weems writes,

> Such rare and unforeseeable moments find me tripping toward a purpose, stumbling upon an insight, backing up into God. When I recognize this Presence, it leaves me incapable of speech, embarrassed by my ignorance, and wanting to take my shoes off — for I know I am on holy ground [*The Other Side*, Philadelphia, 1999].

The word *spirituality* comes from the same root as the word for breath. It literally means "that which gives us breath" or "breathes through us." Our spirituality is that which moves us, which motivates us, inspires us, directs us. It is not external to us but is part of who we are. "It is a cliché that spirituality today is just another commodity, an aspect of consumer choice with its own designer range.... [Ultimately] it will be shaped and formed by that toward which we reach out, for which we yearn" [Kathy Galloway, *The Other Side*, 2004].

I have been moved by the spiritual essence and the yearnings of people I've met over the past few years, while researching stories about healing and hope in preparation for a book entitled *Who Can Heal Us?* [Eleutheria Publishing, 2004]. The book was created by Kathryn Eve and Naureen Shah (a Christian and a Muslim) and myself. We have photographed and collected stories of more than seventy remarkable people living in the city of Toronto. Many of the people we have met are refugees from very different parts of the world. They and their families have come to Canada in the wake of political or economic wars, religious persecution, or natural disasters such as earthquakes, famine, or flood.

Most of those whose stories are told in the book have experienced profound suffering and loss. All are people of religious faith, or with spiritual practices that may not be codified into a set of religious beliefs. Whether Christian, Jew, Muslim, Buddhist, Hindu, agnostic or searcher, these people have taken the raw material of their lives and found meaning and purpose not only in living, but also in starting again. Some have lost family members, jobs, or professions; others, their health and strength. Many have been diagnosed as suffering from post-traumatic stress disorder (PTSD). They are people who have channeled their suffering into art, music, dance, theatre; into writing, political action, justice-seeking, healing.

As a Christian, I have found interviewing these people to be a spiritual encounter, just as I have also found working with clients for thirty years in my profession. The stories of people's lives and journeys have brought into focus for me the question, How do we as human beings make meaning in our lives? What are the symbols that we use to organize into purposeful living our need for community and connection, for being and belonging, as well as for doing?

As a therapist, and as one who trains marriage and family therapists, I am intrigued by the variety of ways in which people search for and experience intimacy — intimacy with self, with others, with God. The word *intimacy* is derived from the Latin *intima*, meaning "inner or innermost." So the sense of touching our innermost core is the essence of intimacy. This is part of what I define as a spiritual quest, and it is heightened today in our society as we witness a renewed hunger for the sacred permeating all areas of post-modern life.

Several factors seem to be fueling an awakening to the importance of taking seriously the spiritual reality of life, among them social isolation, lack of community, long working hours, lack of ability to cope with increased technological advances, an awareness of the ecological crisis, and the desire to reconnect with nature. Books, television programs, tapes and CDs, as well as film and theatre, music and art, are reflecting this societal search for the sacred. Increasingly, sales of books on religion, spirituality, and inspiration are now outpacing other categories.

Counselling and spirituality

There is an increasing demand from church people and clients that not only clergy, but also psychotherapists (including marriage and family therapists) take seriously the spiritual dimension of human experience. Paralleling this is psychotherapy's own evolution toward a bio-psycho-social model of treatment.

More practitioners are now properly recognizing the inextricable interconnectedness of mind, body, and spirit; they understand that reducing human beings to mere biological processes or behavioural programming is misguided. As eminent family therapist William Doherty has pointed out, psychotherapies have often failed in the past to help their clients deal with moral issues. Doherty postulates that "interpersonal morality," the consequences of one's behaviour on the welfare of other people, has been lost in the psychotherapeutic paradigm [*Soul Searching: Why Psychotherapy Must Promote Moral Responsibility*, 1995].

Clergy, therapists, doctors, social workers, and other helping professionals are challenged to be compassionate and hospitable as people come to us and invite us into the sacred space of their life journey of becoming more fully human. Dr. Hugh Drouin, an Anglican who was director of Family Services Ontario, wrote in *Family Times* [Toronto, Winter 2001]:

> People are suffering because they do not feel loved and appreciated and this neglect is eating away at their souls.... As healers, it is our responsibility to keep the doors of our lives and our places of work open to expressions of love and support. If we are compassionate and sensitive to the needs and inner struggling of others, we will never miss an opportunity to express to them our gratitude and appreciation for the people they are.

And Christian ethicist and therapist James Olthius emphasizes that "the art of counselling is not something we do to others, but something we do together." He sees any helping relationship, and the process of therapy itself, as being "an emotional-spiritual process in which we journey together in the hope of healing" [*The Beautiful Risk*, Grand Rapids: Zondervan, 2001].

In working with families, I am challenged and intrigued by the answers I hear when searching to discover how family members (children included) find meaning. Questions such as *What nurtures your spirit? What gives you a sense of rootedness? What gives you joy?* evoke diverse responses such as art and music, prayer and worship, reading and cooking, laughter and the theatre, my cultural identity, growing things, being with friends, walking in nature, having a family meal, playing with my children, celebrating special events with friends and family.

But one doesn't have to be a professional to be a counsellor to, or within, families. Wise elders, friends, and even the youngest among us can give help and inspire hope at times of darkness, despair, and grief within a family's journey. We all need to be reminded at such times to draw on our deepest reservoirs of faith, courage, and hope, and to know that we are held in the light of God's love.

Families may be the source of one's darkness and pain, but they may also be the centre from which we draw new life. In the words of Thomas Merton, "As long as we are on earth, the love that unites us will bring us suffering by our very contact with one another. Because of this, love is the resetting of a body of broken bones." Often, this is what we do in our families — reset emotional and spiritual "bones" broken by life's hurts and losses.

Life passages

Family life is full of passages from birth to death, from joy to sorrow. It encompasses a wide range of human experiences. Some bring fulfillment, others bring a sense of failure. Children and adults experience various stages of growth — from the dependency of infants, through the search for independence in adolescence, through young adult and mid-life maturity, and into another dependency of old age. Throughout these life cycles, there are times of mourning and rejoicing. In the words of the writer of Ecclesiastes, there is a time for every season. This applies to all stages of life, but is especially pertinent when we consider family life.

> For everything there is a season, and a time for every matter
> under heaven:
> a time to be born, and a time to die;
> a time to plant, and a time to pluck up what is planted;
> a time to kill and a time to heal;
> a time to break down, and a time to build up;
> a time to weep, and a time to laugh;
> a time to mourn, and a time to dance;

a time to throw away stones, and a time to gather stones
together;
a time to embrace, and a time to refrain from embracing;
a time to seek, and a time to lose;
a time to keep, and a time to throw away;
a time to tear, and a time to sew;
a time to keep silence, and a time to speak;
a time to love, and a time to hate;
a time for war, and a time for peace
[Ecclesiastes 3:1-8].

Perhaps the greatest gift that parents and grandparents can
give their children to meet the challenges of life, is the call to
seek the wisdom that comes from God.

The fear of the Lord is the beginning of knowledge;
fools despise wisdom and instruction.
Hear, my child, your father's instruction,
and do not reject your mother's teaching;
for they are a fair garland for your head,
and pendants for your neck
[Proverbs 1:7-9].

Words hold great power in children's hearts and minds. Do we
ourselves speak wisdom, or do we give children stones instead
of the bread of life to nourish their spirits? The Bible encourages us to teach children to love God and to follow God's way of
loving one's neighbour as one's self. If they walk in this path,
children will receive God's wisdom.

My child, if you accept my words
and treasure up my commandments within you,
making your ear attentive to wisdom
and inclining your heart to understanding;

if you indeed cry out for insight,
and raise your voice for understanding;
if you seek it like silver,
and search for it as for hidden treasures —
then you will understand the fear of the Lord
and find the knowledge of God.
For the Lord gives wisdom;
from his mouth come knowledge and understanding
[Proverbs 2:1-6].

How we make sense of, and find meaning in, our own lives is reflected in the stories we tell about ourselves. But when a person loses touch with his or her own story, then they become profoundly lost. This is the experience described by many who become addicts, cut off from their spiritual centre. Alcoholics Anonymous and other Twelve Step programs help people to explore and rediscover their own stories, and to find the confidence to tell others in a safe environment. Letting oneself be known in such a context is a profoundly spiritual experience, and has given renewed life and restored health to thousands who have walked this path of healing.

Each passage of life has its own season of weeping and laughter, mourning and dancing, seeking and losing, breaking down and building up. The infant learning to walk, falling down, getting up again — until the exuberance and joy of mastering each step comes to fruition. The four-year-old child, leaving home for the first time to begin school — tentative at first, afraid of losing the security of the familiar, then learning to laugh and sing with classmates. The primary student making the first faltering attempts at learning to read, until attaining the joyous sense of accomplishment at understanding words and sentences.

The adolescent, seeking independence, finding her first job, and receiving her first paycheque. The young adult, falling in and out of love, being heartbroken, then experiencing the ecstasy of connecting with someone who can become a soul mate. Or perhaps not, and then learning the rich rewards of singleness. The mid-life adult, caught between adolescent children and aging parents, stressed at work and at home, but then finding the renewal of joy that comes with new beginnings. The elderly person, lamenting failing health and lost independence, and grieving the loss of lifelong partners and friends, and learning an acceptance of aging and the generosity of sharing wisdom with younger generations.

God has so beautifully created us that we can experience the diversity of life's passages and never stop growing, learning, rejoicing. This is the essence of our spirituality, of our createdness, of our calling — to know God and enjoy the abundance of God's creation, the dance of life. But the brokenness of the world and our own personal griefs and burdens rob us and defeat us, and we forget the steps of the dance. We gradually lose our sense of wonder and gratitude, and find ourselves vulnerable to anxiety, discouragement, estrangement, and a deep sadness. At such times, when we have forgotten who we are, we need the community of church and the embrace of friends or family to hold us up, and to remind us that we are loved.

Jesus and hospitality

The gift of hospitality is spoken of frequently in the Hebrew and Christian scriptures. We are called to welcome the stranger, to share our possessions with others, to "bear one another's burdens." Jesus himself modelled for us compassion and openness to the outsider, ministering healing and comfort to the marginalized and outcast, to those wounded in body, mind, and spirit. He shared his life with his friends and disciples, and the women and men who followed him were characterized by a common life.

When Jesus saw his disciples turning away any who came to him, he rebuked them. He welcomed the lepers, the tax collectors, and the mothers and children who pushed to see him. He noticed and praised the tithing of a poor widow, and his stories told of a generous father welcoming home a wayward son, of a woman finding a lost coin, and a shepherd searching for a stranded lamb. The gospels reveal that at times of loss and grief, Jesus comforts; at times of resistance and ignorance, Jesus confronts; at times of awareness of brokenness and sin, Jesus forgives; at times of celebration and awakening, Jesus rejoices.

As his followers, we are called to do no less. In our own simple everyday acts, we too can do what Jesus did. When we touch others physically or emotionally or psychologically, when we encourage others and treat them as brothers or sisters within the beloved community, then we are part of the healing dance that Christ came to establish among his followers. When we bring our griefs to the foot of the cross, we are called by Christ to be agents of reconciliation. And within the community of the family, with our partners, our children, our families and friends, we are moved to comfort, confront, forgive, and rejoice.

Beginnings and endings

Life in families challenges us with beginnings, with transitions, and with endings. There is a time for connecting, and a time for establishing boundaries. There is a time for changing, and a time to consolidate those changes. There is a time for moving, and a time for staying rooted. The Christian life, lived in family, is a journey from birth to death, the path weaving at times through rocky terrain, through barren wastelands, and through lush and verdant pastures. But there is always God's sustaining promise:

Even though I walk through the darkest valley,
I fear no evil ...
Your rod and your staff shall comfort me
[Psalm 23].

When a child or spouse rejects us, when we walk through the valley of the shadow of death of a loved one or of a broken relationship or promise, when our hearts feel smashed into a thousand pieces, then God the Comforter comes to guide our path and to sustain in us a glimmer of hope, to feed and nurture us at the banqueting table, to restore our souls.

"Come to me, all you who labour and are heavy laden, and I will give you rest," says Jesus. This, too, applies to life in families. Rest, when we are stretched to the limit; rest, when we are so busy there is no time to relax; rest, when we are discouraged and downhearted; rest, when we are grief-stricken. Whether we are parent, child, sibling, grandparent, aunt, uncle, cousin — we all find ourselves somewhere in a family circle. Is it a welcoming circle? Or does it banish members or erect barricades against life?

Ultimately, our families are sacred circles, created to be places where we learn to face the challenges of life and hear the music of forgiveness. And though at times the music is faint and we stumble and fall, families help us to learn and live the complex steps of the dance that is called Love.

> God, kindle thou in my heart within
> A flame of love to my neighbour,
> To my foe, to my friend, to my kindred all,
> To the brave, to the knave, to the thrall,
> From the lowliest thing that livest,
> To the name that is highest of all
> — Celtic Prayer [*God Under My Roof,* Esther de Waal].

Path Books

A LIGHT TO MY PATH

We hope that you have enjoyed reading this Path Book. For more information about Path Books, please visit our website at **www.pathbooks.com**. If you have comments or suggestions about Path Books, please write us at publisher@pathbooks.com.

Other Path Books

Healing Through Prayer: Health Practitioners Tell the Story by Larry Dossey, Herbert Benson, John Polkinghorne, and Others. Prayer is powerful. In this unique book and video, doctors and patients quote scientific surveys and relate personal experiences of healing through prayer. They provide new conviction to people of faith, and new hope to those seeking healing.
1-55126-229-0, 168 pages, paper $18.95
The Power Within, one-hour video
1-55126-234-7 $29.95

Oceans of Grief and Healing Waters: A Story of Loss and Recovery by Marian Jean Haggerty. With courageous candour and strength, Marian Haggerty tells the story of her journey toward healing from grief, after the death of a loved one. This book can be a wonderful companion for those who are alone and grieving, helping them to understand that they do not journey by themselves.
1-55126-396-3 $16.95

Struggling with Forgiveness: Stories from People and Communities by David Self. These powerful firsthand stories reflect the tremendous range of our experience of conflict and forgiveness: in families, at work, between individuals, within whole societies. They reveal how forgiveness can break the cycle of bitterness, revenge, and violence. There is such possibility for release and healing.
1-55126-395-5 $19.95

Practical Prayer: Making Space for God in Everyday Life by Anne Tanner. A richly textured presentation of the history, practices, and implications of Christian prayer and meditation to help people live a rewarding life in a stressful world.
1-55126-321-1 $18.95
Meditation CD: 1-55126-348-3 $18.95
Audio cassette: 1-55126-349-1 $16.95
Leader's Guide: 1-55126-347-5 $18.95

From Fear to Freedom: Abused Wives Find Hope and Healing by Sheila A. Rogers. This book recounts the spiritual journey of five women as they move from childhood into abusive marriages, and then out into self-realization and freedom. The women share their thoughts and feelings about themselves, their abusers, and God. The book offers practical advice for those who have experienced abuse, and for their friends and family.
1-55126-358-0 $19.95

God with Us: The Companionship of Jesus in the Challenges of Life by Herbert O'Driscoll. In thirty-three perceptive meditations, Herbert O'Driscoll considers the challenges of being human, searches key events in the life of Jesus, and discovers new vitality and guidance for our living. He shows us how the healing wisdom and power of Jesus' life can transform our own lives today.
1-55126-359-9 $18.95